# *Tracking Significant Achievement in*

## PRIMARY ENGLISH

# TRACKING
# *Significant Achievement*

*Series editors: Shirley Clarke and Barry Silsby*

**Marian Sainsbury**

*in* **PRIMARY ENGLISH**

Hodder & Stoughton
A MEMBER OF THE HODDER HEADLINE GROUP

**Also published in this series:**
*Tracking Significant Achievement in Primary Mathematics*
*Tracking Significant Achievement in Primary Science*
*Tracking Significant Achievement in the Early Years*

**Acknowledgement**
Many thanks to the schools, teachers and their pupils who
contributed samples of significant achievement for this
book.

*British Library Cataloguing in Publication Data*
A catalogue record for this title is available from the British Library

ISBN 0 340 65479 1
First published 1996

Impression number  10  9  8  7  6  5  4  3  2
Year                    1999   1998   1997   1996

Filmset by Wearset, Boldon, Tyne and Wear.
Printed in Great Britain for Hodder & Stoughton Educational, the educational
publishing division of Hodder Headline Plc, 338 Euston Road, London NW1 3BH,
by Bath Press, Bath

# Contents

# 1 Tracking Significant Achievement

*by Shirley Clarke*

## The purpose of this book

With the advent of the revised National Curriculum, the focus for teachers' ongoing assessment has been to look for **significant achievement**, as opposed to looking for *all* aspects of achievement, which had been the previous practice.

This book, one of a series of four on significant achievement, aims to establish a coherent and manageable framework for organising ongoing assessment in the classroom, in which significant achievement is the focus. The underpinning principles for this are:

◆ the assessment process must include the child, aiming for the child to become part of the evaluation process;
◆ the assessment process must enhance the child's learning and the teachers' teaching;
◆ all assessment processes should be manageable.

This chapter describes good assessment practice, from the planning stage to assessment and record-keeping. It deals with the issue of defining significant achievement and how to look for it and recognise it.

Chapter 2 looks at good assessment practice within the context of English, so it considers good practice in the teaching of English, organisation and resource provision which will enable significant achievement to take place and to be recognised.

Chapter 3 provides a variety of examples of significant achievement, derived from teachers' work in the classroom, covering the age ranges and the different aspects of significant achievement across Key Stage 1 and 2. It is hoped that, by the time you have read all these examples, you will have a very clear idea of what significant achievement in English might look like.

Chapter 4 sets out typical stages of significant achievement in English. The purpose of this is to provide basic guidance for teachers about which aspects of English are most important and significant in a child's development.

Chapter 5 has a question-and-answer format, covering all the issues that arose in a series of courses and during trialling carried out with teachers. It is followed by a final chapter on 'Getting Started'.

# Defining assessment and its purpose

Mary Jane Drummond (1993) has a definition of assessment which clearly describes the process as it takes place in the classroom. She sets it out as three crucial questions which educators must ask themselves when they consider children's learning. Those questions are:

- *What is there to see?*
- *How best can we understand what we see?*
- *How can we put our understanding to good use?*

'*What is there to see?*' refers to the fact that we need to be able to access children's understanding in the best possible way. We need to be constantly talking to children about their work and maximising the opportunities for them to achieve in the first place and demonstrate their achievement in the second.

'*How best can we understand what we see?*' is the next stage. We need to be able to create a climate in the classroom where teachers are not simply hypothesising about the reasons for children's understanding, but have as much information as possible about a child's understanding, coming from the child itself. We also need to be clear about the learning intentions of every activity, so that we know what we are looking for. We need to be flexible, however, because a child's achievement is not always directly related to the aims of the actual lesson. We need to remember that children learn from all their experiences of life, of which school learning is only a part.

*'How can we put our understanding to good use?'* is the key factor in moving children forwards. If the teacher has answered the first two questions, then the information gathered should give clear indications as to what should be the next move in helping a child to continue to progress.

The purpose of the assessment process is to make explicit children's achievements, celebrate their achievements with them, then help them to move forward to the next goal. Without children's involvement in the assessment process, assessment becomes a judgmental activity, resulting in a one-way view of a child's achievement. Information gathered in this way has minimal use. When shared with the child, assessment information is more likely to result in a raising of standards, because the child is more focused, motivated and aware of his or her own capabilities and potential. Good assessment practice enables children to be able to fulfil their learning potential and raises self-esteem and self-confidence.

'Assessment' can sometimes be used as the term for what is, in fact, record-keeping. It needs to be made clear that the assessment process is that outlined so far; a means of understanding children's understanding. Record-keeping is a follow-up to the assessment process, and needs to take place only when significant achievement has taken place. This will be described in some detail later. Evidence-gathering is part of the follow-up to assessment, and needs to be centred round the idea of a 'Record of Achievement' rather than a 'collection of evidence'. It is neither a statutory requirement (see both DFE/DFEE and SCAA documentation), nor useful to keep samples of children's work at set points in time as proof of National Curriculum attainment, whereas Records of Achievement are a motivating and useful aspect of the assessment process.

# The planning, assessment and record-keeping cycle: a practical solution

## The pre-planning stage

If assessment is to be worthwhile, it is clear that we must first maximise the opportunities for children's achievement, by giving them the best possible learning experiences. This can be achieved by a number of support structures in a school and by planning well in advance of the teaching.

Most primary schools have a 'curriculum framework' showing specific coverage of the Programmes of Study for 'blocked' work (e.g. history, geography, science and sometimes maths topics). These charts show who will cover what and in what term. Knowing what it is you have to cover in this way aids planning and enables a school to set up resources of high quality in order to help teachers at the planning stage. Well managed, good quality topic boxes are an excellent idea, with the following as the ideal contents:

◆ artefacts, maps, charts, videos, reference books, tapes;
◆ teachers' previous plans;
◆ lists of local places to visit (e.g. nearby streets with good examples of Victorian houses) and museums, etc;
◆ lists of local facilities (e.g. loan packs from local libraries, etc);
◆ lists of people who can be used as a resource (e.g. artists in residence, local poets and historians, people who work in the school who have related interests and expertise);
◆ brainstorms of starting-point ideas for contextualising the topic (e.g. 'Colour' can be contextualised by creating an optician's shop in the classroom and covering what is needed through this).

With such resource support, teachers are more likely to create interesting, well-resourced topic plans, resulting in contexts in the classroom which enable children to learn more easily.

## The planning stage

The single most important feature of good planning is to have well thought out learning intentions before any creation of activities. It is traditional practice in primary schools to have only the simplest notion of aims, then to launch into a brainstorm, resulting in a topic web of activities. Very often, it is the creation of so many activities which causes manageability problems for teachers. It can also lead to a ticklist approach, where getting through the activities is more important than responding to the way children react to them. It is children's learning which must be our main concern, *not* our plans or schemes of work. They should support the learning, not hinder it.

I suggest a method of planning which starts with more learning intentions and leads to only a few activities, all of which can be developed in depth, resulting in less superficial learning and a less frantic approach to coverage:

1    Find out what the children already know about the area to be covered, by brainstorm, open-ended problem or concept mapping. Brainstorming can be done with any age group. Simply say *'Next term we will be finding out about the Romans. What do you already know about the Romans?'* The resulting brainstorm will provide vital planning information for the teacher: the differentiation range – from the child who has not heard the word 'Roman' to the child who knows more about Romans than the teacher! Having this means that activities can be planned which will meet the needs of all the abilities in the class if the two extremes have been defined.

2    Read the Programme of Study (PoS) statements.

3    Divide the topic, if necessary, into sub-headings – maybe two or three.

4    Create learning intentions, as follows, for each sub-heading:
  ◆ knowledge (*What do I want the children to know?*)
  ◆ skills (*What do I want the children to be able to do?*)
  ◆ concepts (*What do I want the children to understand?*)
  ◆ attitude (*What do I want the children to be aware of?*)
  ◆ equal opportunities (*What do I want the children to be aware of?*)

Clearly, the last two learning intentions lend themselves much more to geography, history or science topics than to maths topics, say, so should be used where appropriate.

In English, the planning stage is mainly related to the range of experiences that children are offered. Some planning for English can take place at the same time as topic planning. A topic on 'Nutrition', for example, could lead to:

◆ writing out a healthy menu, with attention to the organisation and layout of the information;
◆ a 'radio programme' on tape, reporting on the effect of diet on health, interviewing real experts or children in role, and conveying advice about better eating;
◆ group discussion about whether advertisements for sweets should be allowed, leading to a written discussion in which the arguments for and against are set out and conclusions are drawn;
◆ using a brainstorm, formulate questions to which answers are needed and use information books to find those answers;
◆ plan and give an assembly presentation on nutrition in developing countries, raising some of the moral issues involved.

But not all of English can be dealt with as part of a topic. The scope of the Programmes of Study is broad, and the types of text that children read and write cannot be left to chance. Planning will be needed to ensure that they meet a variety of stories and poems, introduced in a way that allows them to appreciate the special features of each.

Much of reading development will take place on an individual basis, with the provisions of the Programmes of Study applied to each child's individual reading experience and progress. But, by careful planning of what the teacher reads aloud to the class, there can be a steady widening of horizons and the introduction of more unusual or difficult types of writing.

Writing too needs to be planned so that the full range of text types are introduced and full scope is given to the children's imagination. There will be a need for particular sessions in which setting the scene for a story, or writing descriptive poetry, or looking at 'surprise' in stories, will be the focus. More about classroom activities for English is given in Chapter 2.

The next stage is to plan the activities the children will do.

With such carefully defined learning intentions, teachers using this approach have said it makes the choice of activity much more focused than before. This in turn means that the teacher is absolutely clear about the purpose of the tasks children will do – a crucial step towards being able to create an evaluative ethos in the classroom. If the teacher is not clear why children are doing a task, the activity is likely to produce superficial results and a feeling of anxiety on the part of the teacher, who may feel that she does not know exactly what she is supposed to be expecting or looking for.

## Making assessments in the classroom: setting up the assessment dialogue

Once the teacher is sure of the purpose of every task, the next step is to let children into the secret! By this, I mean, in words which they will understand, say why you want them to do the activity (e.g. *'I want you to play this language game because it will help you learn how to sound out your letters. I also want to see how well you can take turns'*). This can be said to the whole class, a group, pairs or individuals, depending on how you set children off. The important thing about this is that it takes no more time than it does for the task itself to be explained; it simply needs to become a habit on the part of the teacher.

It is important that children are let into the secret for two reasons:

◆ First, because knowing the purpose focuses the child towards a particular outcome. Very often, children have no idea why they have been asked to do something, and they can only look for clues or 'guess what's in the teacher's mind' as a means of knowing what is expected of them.
◆ Second, because they are being invited to take more control over evaluating their achievements. If the purpose is known, this is more likely to encourage the child to be weighing up the relative strengths and weaknesses of their work as they are doing it.

With children informed of the purpose of the task, the assessment agenda has been set, because, when children finish their work, or are spoken to in the middle of the task, the teacher can say *'How do you think you have got on with sounding your letters/taking turns?'* I do not mean that there should be a systematic attempt to speak to every child, as that would be unmanageable. Apart from setting children off and concluding a session, most of a teacher's time is spent talking to individual children, by going to see how they are getting on or by their coming to the teacher. So the time *does* exist when children can be asked about their progress. It does not need to be structured, set-aside time, but can become part of the ongoing dialogue teachers have with children all through the day. The 'assessment dialogue' is simply a *different* way of talking to the children. The advantage for the teacher in asking the children how they are doing in relation to the 'shared secret' or learning criteria is that it is a powerful strategy for accessing information about children's progress. This type of questioning invites the child to play an active part in his/her learning. Children who are used to being asked such questions readily respond, giving honest answers, because they know the purpose of the teacher's questions is to help their learning process. The answers children give often put a teacher fully in the picture about the child's level of understanding as well as why something now appears to be understood (e.g. *'I understand this now', 'Lisa helped me with these two', 'I didn't want to work with Sam because I wanted to do it like this'*, etc).

This is the assessment process at its best. It describes the means by which the teacher makes all her ongoing decisions about children's learning and what they need to do next. Most of the insights gleaned from this continuous dialogue simply inform day-to-day decisions and it is unnecessary to record them. However, when significant achievement occurs, there is a need to recognise and record the event.

## Making assessments in the classroom: looking for significant achievement and recording it

Record-keeping must have a purpose. If a teacher is to spend time writing things down, it must be useful to both teacher and child. If record-keeping is focused on children's significant achievement, it fulfils many purposes. First, however, we need to look closely at what significant achievement is.

Significant achievement is any leap in progress. It may be the first time a child does something (e.g. sitting still for more than five minutes), or it may be when the teacher is sure that a particular skill or concept has now been thoroughly demonstrated (e.g. in a number of contexts, shows an understanding of how punctuation helps the reader to follow the ideas in writing). Work with teachers has led us to believe that significant achievement falls into five categories:

◆ **physical skill** (e.g. ability to hold pencil appropriately);
◆ **social skill** (e.g. able to work with another child to plan a story);
◆ **attitude development** (e.g. increased confidence in independent writing);
◆ **concept clicking/conceptual development** (e.g. clear understanding of the need to consider the audience in writing);
◆ **process skill** (e.g. able to read with expression).

These are all examples of possible significant achievement in the context of English. Clearly, what is significant for one child is not necessarily so for another. This is a welcome departure from the style of assessment which puts a set of arbitrary criteria, rather than the child's own development, as the basis of one's judgements. However, National Curriculum criteria are still considered, because the Programmes of Study have formed the basis of the planned learning intentions.

The more examples of significant achievement one sees, the clearer the idea becomes. If a child is a relatively slow learner, it does not mean that the child will have no significant achievement. It simply means that significance has to be redefined for that child. For instance, a child who takes six months to learn how to write her name will have a number of significant events leading up to the writing of the name (e.g. the first time she puts pen to paper, the first time she writes the initial letter of her name, etc). Similarly, a child who always does everything perfectly needs to be given more challenging activities in order to demonstrate significant achievement.

The *context* within which significant achievement can be spotted is usually the ongoing assessment dialogue, although it may be demonstrated by a product, such as a piece of writing the child has done. When significant achievements occur, they can be underplayed in a busy classroom. Children have the right to have *all* their significant achievements recognised, understood and recorded. Recognition consists of simply informing the child (e.g. *'Well done, that is the first time you have set your work out neatly'* ).

Understanding *why* the significant event took place is a crucial part of this process. It consists of asking the child *why* the significant achievement occurred. In trialling with teachers, we found that the child's answer often contradicts what the teacher saw as the reason for the significant achievement. This is an important discovery, because it shows that we must find out, from the child, why the significant achievement occurs if we are to be able to follow up the achievement with appropriate teaching strategies. One example of a piece of work brought to a course on significant achievement demonstrates the importance of finding out why the achievement took place:

6 *Ben chose for the first time to be a scribe in shared writing. Shared writing had been going on for over a year, with children in pairs, so this was significant for Ben. The teacher believed that this had happened because of the context of the story ('Horrible Red Riding Hood' – from the wolf's point of view), and her decision was to do more 'reverse' fairy stories as a way of encouraging Ben. However, when asked to go back and ask Ben why he had done this, the teacher reported that Ben said 'It was because you put me with Matthew, and he's shy, like me.' The implications for the teacher now are considerably different. Clearly Ben is sensitive to the dominance of the child he is working with, and the teacher's way forward now is to consider his pairing more carefully, both for writing and perhaps for other curriculum areas.* 9

The child should be central to the recognition and recording of the comment. During the course of a lesson, when the significant achievement occurs, the teacher, in a one-to-one situation, needs to make much of the event (e.g. *'Well done, Ben. This is the first time you have. . . . Tell me why this happened'*).

# Models of recording significant achievement

In trialling this approach, we decided that any teacher records made should as far as possible be in the possession of the child, in order to have the most impact on the child's learning. Two main types of achievement were identified: where it relates to a **product** (piece of work, drawing, etc) and where it relates to an **event**, with no accompanying work.

The following list outlines the features of good, manageable, formative comments which would appear on the child's actual work, or, if it is an event with no product, on a separate piece of paper which is then slotted in to the child's Record of Achievement:

◆ the date
◆ *what* was significant
◆ *why* it was significant

An example of a comment for significant achievement:

❝ *Ben chose today, for the first time, to be the scribe in shared writing. This is a social skill and attitude development. Ben said he was able to do this because he was working with Matthew, who is quiet, like him.* ❞

A typical child's work would have traditional comments on most of the pages (e.g. *'Well done, Ben'*) and occasional comments *about* the child whenever significant achievement has occurred. The formative comment has many benefits:

◆ The child 'owns' the comment and has witnessed it being written, having been asked to say why the achievement took place.
◆ Parents and other interested parties find it much more meaningful to focus on the times when a significant

formative comment has been written, because they make the progression of the child explicit.

◆ The child and teacher can look back to previous comments at any time, to compare with further progress and to help know what needs to be targetted for the future.

# The Record of Achievement

The Record of Achievement is the place where any notable work is placed. The work should be negotiated between the teacher and the child. Unlike previous 'evidence collections', there is no systematic approach when using a Record of Achievement. It is simply an ongoing collection of any special work done by the child, and has been proved to be a highly motivating aspect of assessment. The Record can contain work or other measures of achievement from both inside and outside the school. Its main purpose is to motivate the child and impact on progress. Unlike the more traditional approach to Records of Achievement, the *teacher*, and not the child, is the main manager of the Record, negotiating with the child and gradually helping him/her to be able to identify significance for him/herself.

# Summary

There are two places, then, where comments are written and placed when significant achievement takes place. **Written work or other products** have the comment written onto them and stay in the child's tray, or may be photocopied and placed in the child's Record of Achievement. **Event-style or non-product significant achievement** (e.g. organising a group of children) has the comment written on a piece of paper (perhaps with a decorated border) which is then placed in the child's Record of Achievement. These records should be accessible to the child, not locked away and owned by the teacher. The ideal system is to have concertina folders in a box in the classroom.

Some teachers find that there are too many pieces of paper involved in *non-product* sheets, so preferred to record achievements in a single booklet for each child. This booklet is stored in the child's Record of Achievement and the child is simply asked to bring it to the teacher when something

new is to be recorded in it. References to *product*-style achievements (e.g. *'See Danny's science work on 16 February'*) can also be made in this booklet or on separate sheets, so that there is then a one-to-one correspondence with all the significant achievements for a child and the number of references in the Record of Achievement. Keeping the comment in the child's exercise book or work without placing it in the Record of Achievement, however, has been found to be just as effective in motivating children. The most important thing is that children's achievements are explicitly recognised and a recording made.

In order to be able to easily access significant achievements in children's workbooks, some teachers place a coloured sticker in the top right-hand corner of the page where the comment had been made. This is not a 'praise' sticker, but simply a marker, which is very effective for being able to see progression quickly, and is especially useful for parents and writing reports.

Later on we describe what happens to the Record of Achievement at the end of each year.

## The summative tracking system

So far, I have described the process of assessment and the accompanying formative record-keeping. However, so that the system is rigorous and children do not fall through the net, there needs to be some kind of summative tracking system. This should not be a burdensome task, so I suggest the following simple mechanism: each half-term, term, or perhaps for a whole year, the teacher takes an A3 sheet of centimetre-squared paper or similar, and writes the children's names down the side and the contexts in which significant achievement might occur along the top. These would be, essentially, the teaching contexts. For example: Reading/Writing/Speaking and listening/Number/Shape and Space/Science topic/etc. The headings could also include the foundation subjects, but the statutory requirement is that records of some kind must be kept for the core subjects only. Bearing in mind our definition of significant achievement, however, it would seem appropriate to include all the teaching contexts, or perhaps have a further heading which simply says 'Other contexts'. A teacher in the early years would probably have different headings, such as Play/Role

Play/Sand and Water/Constructional Play or Creative/ Aesthetic/Social etc. Then, when significant achievement occurs, and the teacher has written the brief formative comment, she keeps track of this by entering the date and a code to show which category of significance occurred (see Figure 1).

| Names | Speaking & listening | Reading | Writing | Number | Topic (Science etc.) | Other |
|---|---|---|---|---|---|---|
| Laura | | | 8/2 Ⓒ | | 16/3 Ⓐ Ⓒ | 4/2 Ⓐ Ⓒ |
| Cassie | 3/3 Ⓢ Ⓐ | 14/2 Ⓐ | 19/3 Ⓒ | 2/4 Ⓒ | 1/2 ⓅⓈ | 15/3 Ⓐ |
| Peter | 4/2 Ⓐ Ⓢ | 18/3 Ⓐ | 21/2 Ⓐ Ⓟ Ⓢ | 1/3 Ⓐ Ⓒ | 16/3 ⓅⓈ | 3/4 Ⓢ Ⓐ |
| Roxanne | | 21/4 Ⓒ | 21/4 Ⓢ Ⓐ | 17/3 ⓅⓈ | | |
| Sam | 3/3 ⓅⓈ | | | | 17/3 Ⓒ | |
| Dean | 12/1 Ⓐ | 10/3 Ⓐ | 28/3 Ⓐ Ⓒ | 17/1 ⓅⓈ | 11/3 Ⓟ | 2/4 Ⓟ |
| Jenny | 8/2 Ⓢ | 8/2 Ⓐ ⓅⓈ | 4/1 Ⓒ | 9/3 ⓅⓈ | 20/3 Ⓒ | 11/3 Ⓐ Ⓢ |
| Danny | | | 18/3 Ⓒ | | 6/2 ⓅⓈ | 9/3 Ⓐ Ⓢ |

Ⓐ Attitude development   Ⓒ Conceptual development   Ⓟ Physical Skill
ⓅⓈ Process skill   Ⓢ Social skill

*Figure 1*

This tracking record can serve a number of functions. At a glance the teacher may see:

◆ a few children who appear to have shown no significant achievement, and therefore need to be focused on, in case they have been missed because they are quiet;
◆ a child who has shown significant achievement in, say, reading, but not in writing, and therefore needs to be checked;
◆ the fact that none of the children has shown any significant achievement in, say, science, which indicates a need for the teacher to rethink the curriculum on offer;

◆ a bright child who appears to have shown no significant achievement, which indicates that he/she needs to be given more challenging, open-ended tasks.

One teacher in her second term of tracking significant achievement found that, on average, she recorded six comments per child in a half-term. Figure 2 shows some of these (these comments were written on the child's work or event sheet, and have only been reproduced in this way for the purpose of this book).

## End-of-year records

Anything passed on to the next teacher needs to be useful to that teacher and able to be read quickly and easily. It is of no use passing on the whole Record of Achievement, because much of the content would have served its purpose and been surpassed by subsequent pieces of work. Good practice, therefore, is to sift the contents down to the last four pieces of significant work – say, one story, one account, one maths investigation and one science investigation. This will be manageable and useful for the next teacher to read. In the case of children with particular learning difficulties, it may be useful to pass on more pieces, perhaps showing the progression across the year.

As well as these pieces, the standard items passed on through the school would accompany them (e.g. reading record, end-of-year report, perhaps 'best fit' National Curriculum levels for each child in the class). Teachers involved in trialling this system felt it unnecessary to pass on the summative tracking matrix, because this is essentially a working document.

# Conclusion

This chapter outlines a framework for assessment which first and foremost puts the child's learning and development first. However, **this system can also meet the statutory requirements**. The following chapters have been carefully constructed to build on this chapter; giving examples of significant achievement, defining it within English itself, and answering the most common questions which teachers ask about looking for significant achievement.

| Yr 2 Name | Speaking / listening | Reading | Writing | Number | Topic | Other |
|---|---|---|---|---|---|---|
| Cassie | (S)(A) Took quite a complicated verbal message, and was able to deal with a query and bring back an answer. | (A) Is now choosing to read 'chapter' books. | (C) Writing consistently with correct sentence formation. | (C) Understanding concept of X and knows 2/5/10 tables – with understanding. | (PS) During experiment about light in relation to seeds. 'How can we water the ones that we have to keep covered?' (in the dark). | (A) Able to cope with 'not knowing' how to do something. She can now accept a challenge. |
| Peter | (A)(S) Co-operating with a partner to prepare for class assembly, and behaving in an appropriate manner during assembly. | (A) Avidly 'reads' books on the carpet, at the start of the school day. | (A)(P)(S) Sitting quietly and persevering with his improved handwriting. | (A)(C) Devising assorted maths problems with common answer (ways to make 8), he really persevered. | (PS) Seeds/light experiment. 'Put one lot of seeds up on the shelf – in the shade. (My Nan has a plant that doesn't get much light, it's in the hall.)' | (S)(A) Managing to play sociably with other children during playtime. |
| Dean | (A) Related own story, coherently, to ancillary. | (A) Enjoying using picture dictionaries to aid word recognition. | (A)(C) Can spell SPACE – verbally and written (other spelling very poor). | (PS) Was able to identify the need for string to aid measurement in a 'maze' problem. | (P) Made excellent – unaided – junk and clay models of a rhino. | (P) Persevering with learning to skip – he can do it! |
| Jenny | (S) Leading a small group discussion whilst making a group poster. | (A)(PS) Reading with good comprehension – completed task related to her reading. | (C) Use of common spelling patterns – what, which – who – when. | (PS) Independently solved 'maze' problem by using variety of measuring mediums – found that thread was easiest. | (C) Demonstrated reason for shadow disappearing/re-appearing when body moves into a shadow. | (A)(S) Giving spontaneous praise to a child with low self-esteem. |

*Figure 2*

Teachers, in trialling, were inspired and delighted by the fact that, at last, with this system, they could make the focus of their assessment practice the total development of the child, where **equal status is given to tiny steps, which might otherwise be seen as trivial, and more traditional demonstrations of progress.** The feedback has been, overall, that although it takes a while to get used to this different approach, the impact on the children's self-esteem and progress, the working atmosphere in the classroom, and children's ability to evaluate and set their own targets is considerable and, for some children, has resulted in leaps in progress which teachers have said would not otherwise have occurred. In their first summer after using tracking significant achievement, teachers said that their end-of-year records had never been easier to write.

It seems appropriate to end with some work from a child

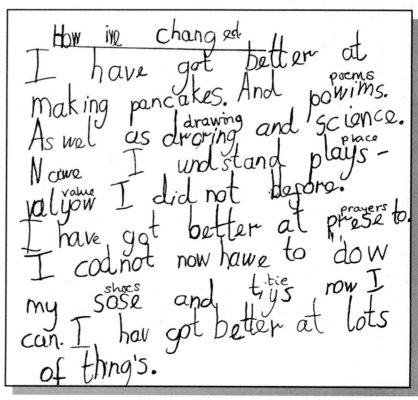

*Figure 3*

(Figure 3). The teacher asked the children, after their first term of focusing on significant achievement, to write a summary of their improvement. I believe that this child's account of his progress (and other accounts were all in the same vein) illustrates perfectly the emphasis that this philosophy places on the whole child, rather than just school-based learning.

## Reference

Drummond, M.J. (1993) *Assessing Children's Learning*, David Fulton Publishers.

# Supporting Significant Achievement in English

## The nature of language in the primary school

Children's language is something they bring with them into school, and use all the time when they are there. They use it to make friends, to make sense of the world around them, to work and to play. They use it all the time in their learning, right across the curriculum. Their speaking and listening, their reading and their writing draw on and reflect the entire curriculum, as well as the children's social relationships and the world outside school. This fact, that language is the medium *through which* pupils experience the world, makes language teaching and learning rather different from other subjects. As teachers, we are developing something that was well advanced before these children even started school.

Language is often discussed in terms of the four modes: speaking, listening, reading and writing. Mostly, children start school able to speak and to listen, but not yet able to read and to write. An important part of our task is, of course, to teach them the skills and strategies they need to succeed as readers and writers. But alongside this, developing language means developing the range of purposes for which language is used, and helping children to accomplish those purposes better. In doing this, their speaking, listening, reading and writing will interact and support each other. Each of the four language modes is an aspect of the child's overall language and should not be seen in isolation. In the course of their classroom work, children will talk about their reading and writing, read their writing, write about their reading, and listen to others reading and talking. Although we might wish to focus on a particular language mode in a particular piece of teaching, the interdependence of the four should not be forgotten.

Language use has real purposes for children. They communicate with others, mix socially, develop and sustain relationships. In reading stories and poems and in taking part in play and drama, they are able to experience other worlds, to imagine how other people feel and think. And language gives access to information of all kinds, across the curriculum and in the outside world. This information is interesting in its own right, and feeds children's curiosity about the world and their understanding of it. These are the real purposes for which children use their language, and their school activities should reinforce and extend their understanding of these purposes.

In the National Curriculum, the Programmes of Study for English deal with speaking and listening, reading and writing separately, but the links between them are also mentioned. Each Programme of Study is set out in three sections: range; key skills; and standard English and language study. The ideas in this chapter relate closely to the Programmes of Study and these sections will be referred to from time to time.

Some children come into school with languages other than English. This knowledge of additional languages is a rich resource that broadens pupils' understanding of language itself and how it works. Their English develops alongside the existing first language. This first language supplies the basic structures of language itself, and actively supports the learning of English. Inevitably, most of the significant achievements discussed in this book will be through the medium of English. But the role of other languages in this should not be ignored, and some of the examples will also point out the achievements in linguistic awareness that can come through knowing more than one language.

# What do we know about learning in English?

Perhaps the most important thing we need to remember about children's learning in English is that, when they start school, their most impressive and significant learning achievement is already behind them. As babies, with only informal help from family and friends, they have mastered the complex and subtle set of rules that allows them to communicate through the medium of language. Even without school, these abilities would continue to develop. An important guiding principle, therefore, is that school learning should acknowledge and build on children's existing understanding of language.

In learning to talk, babies continually try out new sounds and meanings. They rarely manage to produce the correct pronunciation and meaning first time. Instead, their sympathetic listeners interpret, repeat and extend what the baby is trying to say, and the baby gradually revises and practises and comes closer to the way words are used in the adult world.

This ability to try things out, to make approximations and to revise and practise is something that can continue to help children to learn in school, if the child finds in the teacher a sympathetic rather than a censorial audience. This is not to say that children can find everything out for themselves, or that they need only be surrounded by books to learn to read and write. But children will, if encouraged, try out reading and writing for themselves, making guesses where they do not yet have knowledge. As their understanding increases, their guesses will be revised and become closer and closer to correctness. There is a wealth of research evidence showing this development, for example by Margaret Clark, Marie Clay, Ken and Yetta Goodman, Glenda Bissex and Frank Smith.

As teachers, we should be careful not to jump in and correct too eagerly, nor to give an impression that only 'right answers' are acceptable. Making mistakes and correcting them oneself can be a valuable way of learning, but will only take place in a climate where mistakes are accepted as valuable, rather than condemned.

One thing that children are unlikely to have on starting school, however, is very much awareness of their own language use. Their knowledge of language is implicit, rather than explicit: they *use* it, rather than *knowing about* it. They have to be taught that language is something that they can understand, monitor and develop. They need to learn that their talk consists of sentences and words and can be written down using letters and other symbols. This awareness is an essential ingredient of letting children into the assessment secret. They have to 'step back' from their language and to understand it as something that can be described and monitored. The Kingman Report set out in some detail the kinds of discussion about the forms, functions and varieties of language that can help children to become explicitly aware of language use. It is this awareness that features in the 'Standard English and language study' sections of the National Curriculum.

Learning to read and write is a complex activity, because reading and writing are complex abilities. One of the things children have to do is to grasp new knowledge of the conventions by which the sounds of spoken language are represented as written letters. In doing this, they need to associate letters with their typical sounds, and to grasp letter patterns. Usha Goswami's work has shown that the two parts of a word that she calls 'onset' and 'rime' are a useful way to understand how children learn. In a simple word such as *'cat'*, the 'onset' is the initial sound *'c'* and the 'rime' is the whole of the ending, *'at'*. Children can use their knowledge of, for example, *'pink'* to work out *'wink'* and *'sink'*, long before they are able to put together all the individual sounds in the word.

Children also need to learn about the appearance of letters and words. It may seem obvious to us that *B* is the same letter as *b*, but that *d* is not. To a child, though, a *b* looks much more like *d* than *B*.

Alongside these skills, however, and ultimately more importantly, the children have to bring to bear their existing knowledge of language. They must realise that the process is all about making and understanding meaning. They must see reading and writing as valuable in finding things out and in entering the world of the imagination, not as a series of skills without a purpose. Don Holdaway's work has shown how this excitement and enjoyment of language can be part of the child's experience in school. He describes activities such as sharing books, re-telling much-loved stories and playing at writing, and shows how these can be harnessed and used to promote learning.

This points to an essential complexity in the teacher's role. Children will only be able to read and write well when they have *integrated* all the skills, strategies and understanding that they need. Children start from very different points in this. One may have a well developed understanding of story but know little about word and letter shapes and sounds. Another may have been taught letters but have no idea of the role they play in making meaning. Every child will need subtly different teaching in order to develop the different aspects of his or her understanding and to bring them to bear in making meaning. In this, the assessment dialogue has a crucial role to play. When we have a good grasp of the balance of strategies an individual child already possesses, we can judge our teaching to fill the gaps, develop the parts that are underdeveloped and help the child to use the strategies to complement one another. This complex mix is the 'balanced and coherent programme' of key skills in reading that are set out in the National Curriculum Programmes of Study.

As children become more fluent and accomplished readers and writers, the emphasis of teaching and learning shifts. Children are now learning to extend the range of their language accomplishments and to match them carefully to a variety of different purposes. They need to speak and write in different styles for different audiences, and to find a 'voice' of their own, which is at the same time appropriate to the purpose. They will come to read and understand different types of text. As they do this, they will gain greater awareness of the ways language can be used, and the importance of the writer's choice of words.

The teacher's role here, too, is to provide teaching that is matched to each individual child. It may be helping him or her to appreciate a new text type – biography or descriptive poetry, for example. It will certainly include sensitive discussions that will help the child to read 'between the lines' – to bring his or her own experiences and knowledge of the world and literature to appreciate the full meaning of the text. It will also involve a growing awareness of the nature of language, and of variety and choice within language. Children will come to understand that a writer has chosen whether to write in a formal or informal way, or that words are used in advertisements to persuade people to buy things. They will use this knowledge to practise a variety of styles and voices in their own writing.

All of this needs to grow out of the assessment dialogue, so that teacher and child together become increasingly aware of the child's interests and understanding, and work to extend them further. If the teacher regularly talks about who the text is *for* and *why* the words were chosen, children will become able to ask themselves the same question.

# Significant achievement in English

As children learn skills and strategies, make choices about the means of expressing themselves, make judgements about their audiences and carry out their communicative purposes, discussion can make both teacher and pupil aware of progress and learning.

The basic requirements for this dialogue are those for all assessment dialogue, in any subject. The teacher must be prepared to listen to the children and to be a conversational partner, guided by the child, rather than starting with a pre-set agenda. The teacher must have a firm belief in the value of mistakes as learning and assessment tools, and have enough trust in the children to allow them to learn through their mistakes. And in all this, there is the need to make children consciously aware of what they take for granted: their abilities in language.

As in all subjects, the significance of achievement will vary from child to child. But the overall aim in language development is the *communication of meaning.* Perhaps the easiest misconception in identifying significant achievement in English is to concentrate excessively on isolated skills, as these are the most straightforward to recognise. It is easier to decide whether a child knows the sound 's' than to observe how far that child can integrate this knowledge with other understanding in gaining meaning from a text. But ultimately, it is the gaining of meaning from the text that is important. Along the way, there will surely be isolated skills that are worth noting, but the emphasis must remain firmly on meaning and understanding, purpose and audience, or the assessment dialogue will be trivialised and record-keeping become unwieldy.

There are types of speaking, listening, reading and writing that are only found, or most often found, in other areas of the curriculum. Significant achievement in English can therefore be distinguished right across the curriculum, and the purpose of a task might well be a cross-curricular one – for example, showing what you know about reflection of light *and* showing how to organise information when writing about science, or how to draw information from various sources in history *and* present that information clearly and coherently.

# Development in English

This section shows some broad lines of development in the five areas of significant achievement that were distinguished in Chapter 1: physical skills, social skills, attitude development, concept clicking and process skills. The kind of development that can be expected is described very generally here, and then, in Chapters 3 and 4, a range of examples will be given to illustrate this in more concrete terms.

## Physical skills

FROM . . .
. . . forming letters recognisably

TO . . .
. . . varying handwriting style according to purpose; presenting letters, posters, stories, poems, etc, appropriately and attractively.

## Social skills

FROM . . .
. . . talking with small numbers of familiar children and adults

. . . asserting a point of view

. . . involvement in imaginative play

TO . . .
. . . talking with groups of various sizes, of known and unknown people.

. . . listening to others
. . . adjusting ideas, making suggestions, giving and receiving constructive criticism.

. . . taking a variety of roles, including some unfamiliar or unsympathetic ones.

## Attitude development

FROM . . .
. . . enjoyment of familiar books

. . . writing in one or two familiar forms

. . . talking and writing for oneself

TO . . .
. . . enjoyment of a range of types of book.

. . . willingness to try out new types of writing.

. . . talking and writing for others, judging what information they need and how to interest and entertain them.

## Concepts

| FROM . . . | TO . . . |
| --- | --- |
| . . . using language unreflectively | . . . knowing that language consists of words and sentences, that the choice of words can be controlled for effect. |
| . . . print as mysterious black marks on the page | . . . knowledge of letters, written words, the relationship between spoken and written language. |
| . . . understanding stories | . . . discerning character, plot, theme, style, being able to discuss and write about them and their contribution to enjoyment. |

## Process skills

| FROM . . . | TO . . . |
| --- | --- |
| . . . using some reading strategies | . . . having a good grasp of all reading strategies, and using them fluently as needed. |
| . . . knowing some spelling patterns | . . . knowing how to spell most words and knowing which words need to be checked; knowing how to learn spellings. |
| . . . not understanding what punctuation is for | . . . understanding what punctuation is for . . . using all forms of punctuation fluently and appropriately. |
| . . . expressing a point of view | . . . knowing how to learn through talking with others. |
| . . . writing as an immediate form of self-expression | . . . using note-taking, brainstorming, drafting, revision as appropriate. |
| . . . reading with literal understanding | . . . reading with deeper understanding, appreciating layers of meaning, understanding nuance and implied meanings. |

# Creating a climate for learning in English

There are clear implications for classroom practice in what has been said so far. This section will draw out some of these implications and offer suggestions for practical classroom approaches that follow on from them. The overall aim is to retain in school the freshness and authenticity that children's language already has. Children should read and write, speak and listen because they see the point in it, because it answers to their real purposes. Their progress in all these activities can be tracked through the assessment dialogue.

Because purposes need to be real, and because children are all different, this implies scope for *choice* in their language activities. As far as possible, children should be allowed to read and write, talk and listen, about things that interest them and that fire the individual imagination. Of course, this does not mean a completely 'hands off' approach on the part of the teacher: children need to be helped to *extend* the range of the reading, writing, speaking and listening that they enjoy. The teacher should regularly be asking questions such as:

◆ *What about telling another group about what you have found out?*
◆ *Would you like to write a letter to children in another school?*
◆ *How about writing a newspaper article for a change?*
◆ *Have you looked at these new books?*
◆ *Let's see how to find out what we want in this book.*
◆ *Can you tell the children in this group why you like this book?*
◆ *Ask your friend to tell you about his favourite poem in this book.*

Choice itself is an important part of attitude development. It must be part of the assessment dialogue, to be monitored and developed on an individual basis, not imposed upon the class en masse by the teacher. Noticing what children choose, and when they extend the range of that choice, will be an important part of your assessment information.

# Reading

The classroom collection of books is a precious resource and deserves careful thought. How are the books chosen? Are the children involved in the choice? The books need to be organised and classified in a way that all the children understand and can use. *Range* of reading matter is crucial, as the National Curriculum Programmes of Study make clear – are there stories and poems on different topics and themes? . . . reflecting a variety of cultural backgrounds? . . . written in different ways? Are there some picture books and some books without pictures, in all age-groups? Are there books about all the other main curriculum areas? . . . reference books? . . . books that will help children to understand their feelings and relationships? The books need to be changed thoughtfully from time to time, and here the children's involvement gives opportunities to talk with them about their choices.

Books *made* in school are an important part of any class book collection. Some examples are:

◆ re-tellings of favourite class stories, perhaps with changed characters or endings;
◆ celebrations of the languages known by children, with a greeting, or the numbers, or the alphabet, in each;
◆ books with photographs of class events, outings or topics, with a commentary;
◆ 'guide books' of the school, or the classroom, or particular displays or activities;
◆ books made by older children for younger children.

Along with a rich, well-organised book corner, reading must be given status as a classroom activity. It is all too easy to fall back on reading as a fill-in activity, when 'work' is finished, but this undermines its importance. Many classes have silent reading time, and many schools have 'ERIC' – 'Everyone Reading In Class' – or similar sessions, when the whole school, teachers, pupils and visitors, read together. But in addition to this, children need to be given time to browse on their own or with friends, and to read alone or with others, as a legitimate and valuable piece of class work. These opportunities can be accompanied by discussion and by structured teaching from time to time, helping children to share books and to articulate how they choose and use them:

◆ *Today we're going to look at these information books and find out what they can tell us.*
◆ *I'd like you all to choose a poem and share it with a friend;*
◆ *Why did you choose that book?*
◆ *What do you think it is going to be about? What makes you think that?*
◆ *Have you read any other books by this author?*
◆ *How are these books the same? How are they different?*

One way of doing this is to have 'literature circles' where a group of children read the same book and then come together to discuss it.

In teaching children the first stages of reading, individual reading and discussion with the teacher has an obvious importance. It is in this individual conference that teacher and child note the strategies the child is using successfully, and the child's interest in and understanding of events, characters, pictures, humour, information. But there are other, less teacher-intensive ways of teaching reading strategies, of drawing children's attention to the detail of the print. Using a big book with a group of children, for example, the teacher can cover up one of the words and use this to model reading strategies:

◆ *Which words would make sense here?*
◆ *Is there any rhythm or rhyme that will help us to predict?*
◆ *What happens if we read on, beyond the blank?*
◆ *Now look at the first letter: what sound might this be?*
◆ *Which words could begin with this letter?*
◆ *Where have we seen this letter pattern before?*

and so on, demonstrating the integration of meaning, sentence structure, sounds and visual patterns. This makes explicit the thought processes that children need to make automatic in their reading and provides a shared vocabulary for discussing progress.

As children become independent readers, the reading conference will shift in its emphasis, so that discussion might include:

◆ *How is this book similar to others you have read?*
◆ *How does it contrast with others?*

◆ *Why do the characters act as they do?*
◆ *What do we know about when and where the story is set? How do we know this?*
◆ *How does this story or poem make you feel towards its subject-matter? How does the author arouse these feelings?*
◆ *What information does this text give you? How is it organised? How can you best read it to find out what you need? What organisational devices are there to help you?*
◆ *What is this article or advertisement trying to do? What effect is it aiming for? How does it achieve this?*

Some of the work done by David Wray and his associates suggests ways of helping children to understand what they read across the curriculum. This research draws attention to the importance of preparing for reading information texts, by outlining existing knowledge and by formulating questions. There are also ways of presenting the information so that children are encouraged to read for meaning rather than just copying out the text.

There are many ways of helping children to develop a personal response to reading besides discussion. Try:

◆ imaginative play or structured drama;
◆ rewriting it from another angle (*Horrible Red Riding Hood*);
◆ writing part of the story as a diary entry, newspaper report, play script, argument, letter;
◆ interviewing one of the characters to find out about motives and feelings.

These responses can be developed individually, or with a group of children working independently, or as a group activity with teacher in role, as facilitator, model or scribe, depending on the maturity of the children.

# Writing

Children need to see writing as an activity in which they can exercise choice and express their interests, imagination and curiosity. If possible, they should not always write in exercise books, but have some scope for variety. For example, you might provide paper and pens of different shapes, sizes and colours. Tiny books of just a few pages are often popular, especially with beginner writers. These can be made of scraps of paper that would otherwise have been thrown away. Ensure that imaginative play areas, investigatory and construction activities have note pads and pencils. With older children, you might spend some time looking at calligraphy and illuminated letters and encourage experimentation with writing styles; or teach bookbinding as a technology activity and encourage pupils to make their own book-corner books.

Identify audiences for the children to write for. It is only by having a real reader that children will understand what the reader needs to know. For example:

◆ writing for each other: instructions for making models, recipes, accounts of successful investigations, recommendations of books, guides to display areas;
◆ making story books for the book corner;
◆ considering the needs of visitors to school and classroom;
◆ writing for a variety of adult audiences, in school, at home and by letter.

At the same time, children should feel able to write for themselves sometimes, to organise their thoughts or explore their feelings without needing to consider audience or correctness. In discussion, you can make them aware of the different demands of different audiences, so that they learn to think this through for themselves. In writing, too, the emphasis in the National Curriculum Programmes of Study is on the range and variety of the types of writing children are asked to do, as well as the way they go about it. Here, too, David Wray's work has some interesting suggestions, and the National Writing Project has provided many insights for helping children to understand the range available to them.

# Speaking and listening

Children are natural talkers and listeners, but it is misleading to take this to imply that oracy can be left to develop on its own. It is also a mistake to see teacher-led class discussion as the main forum for speaking and listening activities – although, of course, it has a part to play. Much more difficult, but very important, is the need to help children to talk cooperatively and constructively about their work – discussing books they have read, for example, or carrying out an investigation in mathematics or science, discussing an artefact in history or working together with a computer. The crucial point here is to make children aware that the ability to discuss is something they can cultivate, something to be learned, something they can monitor and assess. Ask:

◆ *How do you think your discussion went?*
◆ *Did you all listen to the others? Take turns?*
◆ *Did anyone take up a suggestion somebody else had made?*
◆ *What did you learn from each other?*
◆ *How could you have said that differently?*

Notice how the groups interact, and try to ensure that nobody is too dominant or too withdrawn. Gradually, children will become better at disagreeing constructively, at being assertive when they believe they are right. Respect for others, collaboration and constructive criticism can be modelled and discussed, monitored and commended.

In speaking and listening, too, there is a sense of audience and purpose to be developed. Talk can be more formal or less formal, depending on the occasion. The audience may have a good deal of knowledge about the topic, or it may be completely new to them. The level of information to be given, the vocabulary used and the degree of detail must be judged carefully. As with writing, it is important to identify specific, real audiences – individuals, small groups, classes, occasionally the whole school or an audience of adults – and to match the presentation to the needs of that real audience. The work of the National Oracy Project provides many suggestions for developing work in speaking and listening.

## Using mistakes positively

Another important message from what we know about children's language learning is a positive attitude to *mistakes*. If treated sensitively, pupils' mistakes can be a key to their learning and to their ability to become aware of their own progress. The ultimate aim is that children should be able to read and write, spell and punctuate correctly. But on the way to achieving that aim, it is counter-productive if a child feels that he or she should only set pen to paper, or should only attempt to read, when certain of being correct. Mistakes are an important learning tool and a window into the child's understanding. In discussing mistakes, the teacher needs to convey this complexity, and to help the

children, too, to see their mistakes in a positive light –
whilst still recognising that they *are* mistakes. Try saying:

◆ *You have got nearly all the letters right in this word; there's
  only one you need to change; which one is it?*
◆ *Yes, that word makes sense here, but look more carefully at the
  letter pattern.*

In talking about language activities, too, we need to find
ways of helping children to become aware of their own
language use:

◆ *Can you find a different word to use here, instead of repeating
  the same one?*
◆ *Can the reader understand what happens next? How would
  you make it clearer?*
◆ *How does the writer make you feel scared? sad? excited?
  Which words did the writer choose to do this?*

By talking about language, children will gradually learn how
to step back from their own communication and to monitor
and revise their language skills.

This chapter has concentrated on the need to set up
classroom activities so that children's language development
in school is rich and varied, meaningful and progressive. In
such a climate, the assessment dialogue can thrive, and
teacher and child together can discuss and plan progress.
Chapter 3 will give some examples from real classrooms,
with teachers working in this kind of way and noting
significant achievement when it occurred.

# Further information: quotations and references

6 *By far the most surprising and significant aspect of pre-school book experience, however, is the independent activity of these very young children with their favourite books. Almost as soon as the infant becomes familiarised with particular books through repetitive readings, he begins to play with them in reading-like ways.* 9

Don Holdaway

6 *Like other inventive spellers, Paul at five years old represented the short 'e' sound with the letter 'a'. . . . A week later, as he read the print on a red raspberry yogurt container, he observed that he had spelled 'red' RAD, which he now understood was not right because, as he explained, RAD said 'raid'. Thus, at five years old, Paul was aware of his own learning, was able to note differences between his own and conventional spelling systems, and was able to explain why his was incorrect.* 9

Glenda Bissex

6 *The teachers of classes achieving high standards generally ensured that the children had a wide variety of good reading material in addition to any published scheme or schemes adopted by the school. Moreover the breadth of reading material in these classes was not left to chance. The teachers planned children's reading activities so that they encountered, for example, a good variety of fiction and poetry, read for information from book and non-book sources, read their own and other children's writing, read instructions, signs, maps, lists, indexes, directories, newspapers, magazines, advertisements and read out loud to address others in such gatherings as school assemblies.* 9

HMI Report: *The Teaching and Learning of Reading in Primary Schools*

❝ *The teacher needs*

◆ *respect for and interest in the learner's language, culture, thought and intentions;*
◆ *the ability to recognise growth points, strengths and potential;*
◆ *the appreciation that mistakes are necessary to learning;*
◆ *the confidence to maintain breadth, richness and variety, and to match these to the learner's interests and direction (i.e. to stimulate and challenge);*
◆ *a sensitive awareness of when to intervene and when to leave alone.* ❞

David Allen, National Association of Advisers in English, quoted in *English for Ages 5 to 11* (The Cox Report)

❝ *English should develop pupils' abilities to communicate effectively in speech and writing and to listen with understanding. It should also enable them to be enthusiastic, responsive and knowledgeable readers.* ❞

National Curriculum Programmes of Study: General Requirements for English

## References

Barrs, Myra and Thomas, Anne (eds) (1991) *The Reading Book*, London: Centre for Language in Primary Education.

Goelman, Hillel, Oberg, Antoinette and Smith, Frank (eds) (1984) *Awakening to Literacy*, Portsmouth, NH: Heinemann Educational Books (contains articles by Margaret Clark, Marie Clay, Ken and Yetta Goodman, Glenda Bissex, Frank Smith and many others).

Goswami, Usha and Bryant, Peter (1990) *Phonological Skills and Learning to Read*, Hove: Lawrence Erlbaum Associates.

Holdaway, Don (1979) *The Foundations of Literacy*, Sydney: Ashton Scholastic.

Meek, Margaret (1990) *On Being Literate*, London: Bodley Head.

Robinson, Muriel and King, Carole (1995) 'Creating communities of readers', *English in Education*, *29*, 2.

White, Janet and Karavis, Sylvia (1994) *The Reading Repertoire at Key Stage 2*, Slough: NFER.

Wray, David (1994) *Aspects of Extending Literacy*, Exeter Extending Literacy Project.

# 3 Significant Achievement in the Classroom

This chapter is, in more ways than one, the centre of the book. In it, there is a collection of work from a wide variety of classrooms showing significant achievements from children across the whole primary age range.

The work comes from different children, with different backgrounds and different learning experiences. It illustrates some of the approaches to classroom practice outlined in Chapter 2, and it demonstrates the features of significant achievement described in Chapter 1. The examples here are not exceptional pieces of work produced in extraordinary conditions. They are ordinary pieces of classroom work, but pieces that the teacher has noticed because they are important in a particular child's development. It will be clear from these examples that something significant for one child may not be significant for another.

Each example starts by saying what happened – a description of what took place, or the child's work itself, or, sometimes, the teacher's and child's record of the achievement. As much of this book is about speaking and listening or reading, many of the achievements took place in discussion between teacher and child, so there is no written product. It is important to remember that ephemeral evidence of this kind is necessary, as well as written work, in a recording system.

Following the example itself, there are four important additional pieces of information. The first is the reason why this event was significant for this child. The second is the child's view of why it happened. The third is an indication of the type of achievement – physical, social, attitude, concept or process. Finally, the 'comment' section draws out implications for teaching, and also relates this example to other points made throughout this book, drawing together the relationship between assessment, curriculum and these examples.

The examples are arranged starting with the youngest children. Examples of speaking, listening, reading and writing are intermingled, as are physical, social, attitudinal, conceptual and process achievements.

# Leslie (Reception)

Leslie spoke in class for the first time.

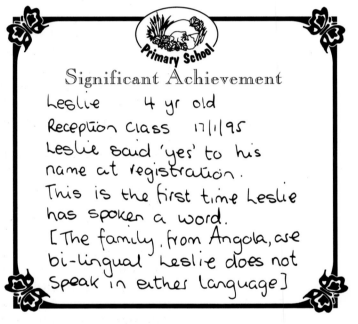

Significant Achievement

Leslie     4 yr old
Reception Class    17/1/95
Leslie said 'yes' to his name at registration.
This is the first time Leslie has spoken a word.
[The family, from Angola, are bi-lingual. Leslie does not speak in either language]

**Type: social skill and attitude development**

## Comment

This example shows how a school can recognise and record significant achievements even when there is no written product. Leslie's certificate records an important step in his social and attitude development as, for the first time, he has the confidence to speak in class. This is a case where we cannot ask Leslie directly what led to this achievement, but Leslie's teacher will continue to provide him with a secure environment where his talking can flourish. His language development will be reinforced by plenty of practice with shared books, rhymes and songs and by some repetitive work with the whole class requiring the same answer, such as *'big'* or *'little'*.

# Vicky (Reception)

In Vicky's class, there is a board with the children's names which says *'at home'* and another board which says *'at school'*. When the children get to school, each one gets the correct name and puts it on the correct board. Vicky recognised her name.

## Why was this significant?

Vicky had not previously recognised her name.

## Why did it happen?

Vicky said *'I just remembered from yesterday.'*

## Type: concept clicking

## Comment

This was an important step in Vicky's conceptual development, as she recognised the shapes of the letters in her name, realising for the first time that spoken words can be written down in predictable ways. Her teacher noted that she needed continuing support and praise for a while as she found her name each day. Gradually, this understanding will extend to the words Vicky encounters in her favourite books.

# Helen (Reception)

Helen was asked to work with a group in producing a book, after much discussion about how to make one. Helen asked if she could make one on her own. Her book was exceptional.

## Why was this significant?

Helen had not produced work of this quality before.

## Why did it happen?

Helen said *'I knew I could make one on my own after seeing them.'* Her teacher noted that she was very motivated and excited by the book-making, so the meaningful context enabled her to excel herself in her writing.

## Type: **physical skill** and **attitude development**

## Comment

This is an example of a physical skill and also a development in attitude, as Helen gained the confidence and motivation to do well. It is clear that an awareness of other children helped Helen to take this step forward, and the influence of other children in significant achievement can be seen in several of the examples.

# **Kate** (Reception)

Kate had done a drawing and when her teacher asked what it was, she said *'It's a monster.'* Her teacher said *'Can you have a go at writing that for me?'* and Kate wrote:

tisomasstr

## Why was this significant?

This was the first time Kate had done unaided writing.

## Why did it happen?

Kate said *'I just guessed.'*

## Type: **process skill** and **attitude development**

## Comment

This shows a gain in Kate's confidence in her process skills. It demonstrates how children can learn through having a go, without worrying unduly about getting everything right. It also gives her teacher a fascinating insight into what Kate knows about letters and words. She knows the letters of *'it's'*, but puts two of them the wrong way round. She knows the word *'a'*. She knows most of the consonant sounds in *'monster'*, at the end as well as at the beginning. Children very often know their consonant sounds before the vowels. It would probably help Kate for her teacher to focus on pointing out the spaces between words when they are reading together.

## Gary (Reception)

Gary wrote his first word: ball.

**Record of Achievement**

Gary was painting -
He made a "round-line"
picture and asked if
he had spelt 'ball'.
correctly - He had painted
b, a, and l, l.
He says it is because he
is learning to spell with
his brother Simon.

**Type: concept clicking**

## Comment

This important achievement shows that Gary has grasped the concept that words can be written down, and that he has noticed and learned the letters of the word *'ball'*.

# Simone (Year 1)

Simone brought her reading book up to her teacher and read it clearly, fluently and with expression.

## Why was this significant?

She had previously lacked confidence in reading and this was a significant difference.

## Why did it happen?

Simone said *'I can read it because I heard Joanne reading to you yesterday.'*

**Type: process skill and attitude development**

## Comment

Simone's achievement is an advance in the process of reading, and also in attitude, as she has the confidence to read for herself. She needs to hear the same story read many times, to create a model for her own reading. She will then continue to have the confidence to read for herself books that she knows well. This will be one of the foundations of her independent reading.

# Peter (Year 1)

Peter one day surprised his teacher by announcing that he was going to bring in some magic tricks to show. He dressed up in cloak and top hat, and performed several tricks well, accompanied by the appropriate patter.

## Why was this significant?

Peter, who speaks another language at home, was usually shy and unable to relate to other children. This was a confident performance in front of the whole class.

## Why did it happen?

When asked why he was suddenly brave enough to do this, Peter said that he wanted to show his magic to his friends. His teacher also noted that he was capitalising on a skill he knew he had, and that the magician's outfit worked as a kind of disguise to give him confidence.

Type: **social skill** and **attitude development**

## Comment

This very considerable achievement in Peter's social development can be followed up with plenty of drama and role-play work, perhaps using other costumes and props. His particular contribution might be recognised by setting up a 'magic area' for a while in the classroom.

# Lisa (Year 1)

Lisa wrote unaided for the first time about crossing the road.

### Why was this significant?

Lisa had previously lacked confidence in writing, asking for every single word.

### Why did it happen?

Lisa said *'I was trying to do what James was doing and James doesn't use a word book. Using a word book slows you down.'* This was the first time she had sat beside James.

**Type: process skill and attitude development**

## Comment

Lisa is now ready to have a go with her writing, trying out words for herself and showing her teacher how much she already knows about written language. This step forward in process and attitude again shows the importance of the influence of other children, like Helen and Simone above. Lisa's teacher decided that as peer influence was so motivating for her, Lisa should sit with children who help to give her positive self-esteem, like James.

# David (Year 1)

David read a story to his teacher with expression.

## Why was this significant?

David was a faltering reader, lacking fluency and expression.

## Why did it happen?

David said *'Because I knew the story.'* His teacher noted that the story had been read to the children several times. This gave David the confidence to read it. He had many cues and was also able to model the teacher's expressive reading.

## Type: **process skill** and **attitude development**

## Comment

David's achievement demonstrates the importance of allowing early readers to become familiar with favourite books and to read the same story repeatedly. The stories which are read to the class need to be part of the book store from which individual children read. Listening to the teacher, and playing at reading with friends, work alongside learning words and sounds in building up the ability to read fluently.

# Sophie (Year 1)

Sophie spent a considerable length of time writing two pages retelling the story of Little Red Riding Hood. She volunteered to read her work to the class and was able to do so without hesitation.

can ried Lletru Rud RIn'
tGo 2s Lick His Once
uront ime ter was
a Lie tru Glruc rnd Llet(e
Red RIng Hrd
ø DAY Hr uo mruclrd
Llet rome Red Renl ng Hred
crlti Yow Go to Yow Gdrn mous
BE crrs yow a drmmow
IS In bed and she Is
illel Sor Yow
r Go too tuack
srm Crrs and sorn
wr and ashe frr
and she Hrew rx
She Chm to the
Wood

Seh Kam to the BIG
Bid WrF
was
Yo name crnalee My
name is Ll e trme
Red RIng Hld PIc
Slm Fnless i Soshe dile
the wrmf wt thetoght cint
he cAm to the Glld mt he wa s in
bed nooc nooc went itln
and Glld uP the Old Gnr
and gll t in to bed then
et me Red RIIng Hlh Cam
c nooc went Lletrme
kling Hlld She cam In
e sld wut BIG ells
w Glt oo the
to SEE yow in m BIG llefyow it oll t
Hume cam ani cut Hem ur and ot cot Grn and
the EG

## Why was this significant?

Sophie's writing was usually limited to one or two sentences.

## Why did it happen?

Sophie said that it was because she was so pleased to find out that she was able to write the story entirely unaided.

**Type: process skill and attitude development**

## Comment

Sophie's work shows an increase in confidence in the process of writing. Compared with Lisa, above, Sophie has moved from being willing to write one or two sentences to realising that she can write a whole story of two pages. This example again shows the importance of familiarity with stories in supporting children's own reading and writing. Sophie knows the story conventions *'Once upon a time . . .'* and *'One day . . .'* She tells the whole story in sequence. She has put direct speech and sound effects *('nooc nooc')* into her narrative. Her invented spellings have many of the consonant sounds correct, so that her meaning can be followed and she was able to read back her own work. As well as plenty of other experiences of stories, Sophie is probably ready now to begin to learn about the way full stops help the reader to follow what she has written.

# Gareth (Year 1)

Gareth made a scrap-book, decorated the cover and brought it to show his teacher. He said *'I've put a house on the front because I want it to look nice.'*

Record
of
ACHIEVEMENT

Gareth made his scrap book, and finished it during one session. The first time he has worked all the way though. He asked for help and did not waste time - he drew a good house on the front "because I want it to look nice". He says he did it nicely because he wants to be good at work.

### Why was this significant?

This was the first time Gareth had worked through a session without losing concentration. The house was a particularly good drawing.

### Why did it happen?

Gareth said *'It's because I don't want to be naughty – because I want you to be pleased.'* He had previously made an art-straw model of a house which was still on display.

### Type: attitude development

### Comment

This is an important advance in Gareth's attitude – he wants to do well, is confident that he can, and concentrates as a result. He needs to continue to have plenty of practical experiences that will allow him to succeed, and he also needs plenty of praise.

## Carol (Year 2)

For the class topic, the children had to write a postcard to one of their relatives, requesting a postcard of the local area to be sent back. Carol had no far away relative, so she wrote to a friend of the teacher's. Her postcard, which she wrote and drafted in one day, is shown opposite.

### Why was this significant?

Carol disliked writing and normally took a long time to finish work.

### Why did it happen?

She said *'I want to get a postcard back.'*

### Type: process skill and attitude development

### Comment

Carol gives a clear example of one of the points made in Chapter 2. She finds motivation in writing because her teacher gives her a real purpose. Suddenly writing becomes

> 11.11.94
> cla$---
>
> Dear Kieron,
>
> I would like to
> come to your house. I
> would like to play golf
> with you. I am seven
> years old. I have three
> brothers.
>
> from Carol
> x x x x x x

something you do to communicate with someone far away, and no longer a chore. Carol needs to be given other real-life purposes so that her attitude and skill can continue to develop.

## Mohammed (Year 2)

Mohammed, whose home language is Turkish, told this story to his support teacher, who scribed for him:

  ❝ *The boy looks like a king. On his head he wears a crown. He is eight years old and today it is his birthday. His hair is black and short. The boy's name is Sam.*

    *Sam goes walking in the woods and he sees a man doing magic. Sam says 'Why are you doing magic?' The magician says 'Because I am looking for a boy.'*

    *Sam goes with the magician to his house. He sees magic things, he sees magic pencils and magic books. There is a cat and a dog in the house. The walls are painted red and green. In one of the rooms there is a snowman. ,*

## Why was this significant?

This was the most that Mohammed had ever said when working one-to-one, and shows his enjoyment and understanding of stories for the first time.

## Why did it happen?

Mohammed said, through a Turkish parent, that he likes telling stories and knew that he had done well. His grandfather has a book of stories in Turkish which he reads to Mohammed.

Mohammed's teacher identified several aspects of teaching that helped Mohammed to do well. The class were given a story plan, to be written one chapter each week, and this encouraged Mohammed to put his understanding about stories to full use. His support teacher was very clear about what the outcome was to be, because of the clear structure of the activity. This allowed her to question him in a skilful way, drawing out the vocabulary to fit the activity.

**Type: process** and **social skill**

## Comment

This is a good example of the way the home language supports development in English. Mohammed's understanding of story – character, structure and the 'magic' genre – comes mainly through hearing Turkish stories at home. But he is able to put this rich background knowledge to use as his spoken English develops.

# Lee (Year 2)

Lee read *The Go Cart* particularly well. He wanted to write a line from the story in the book, and wrote *'They had a . . .'*. He told the teacher he wanted to write the word *'fight'*. She showed him how to write the word and got him to say words that rhymed with *'fight'*. The next day he used magnetic letters to make the words *fight*, *sight*, *night* and *right*.

## Why was this significant?

Lee was usually a poor reader and speller.

## Why did it happen?

Lee said *'Because of the story.'* He enjoyed the story and was motivated by the story line.

**Type: concept clicking**

## Comment

This example shows the 'clicking' of an important concept which will help Lee with both his reading and his writing. By making him focus on the rhyming *sounds* of words, his teacher helped him to make the connection between this and the *visual pattern* of the letters that are used to write the sound – part of the 'phonic knowledge' in the National Curriculum Programmes of Study.

# Emma (Year 2)

Emma had had difficulty holding a pencil properly. One day she stood up in class and said *'I can do it!'* She subsequently wrote her first unaided story.

### Why was this significant?

Emma had been given a pencil grip, and various other pencils designed to improve her grip, and nothing had worked.

### Why did it happen?

Emma explained that one of her teachers had given her a special pencil (a novelty pencil) and she had been taking it home and practising with it. She was able to write the story because *'Well, I can write now I can hold the pencil.'*

**Type: physical skill** and **attitude development**

### Comment

In Emma's case, there is a clear interaction between the physical skill of using a pencil, and the much broader activity that is 'writing'. For Emma they are indissolubly linked, so that the lack of the physical skill forms a block on the entire process of writing for her. Emma's teacher noted the contrast between the learning aids Emma had been given, which seemed to make her self-conscious, and the novelty pencil, which worked by giving her motivation. Children's confidence can sometimes be boosted by quite unpredictable factors, as Emma's was.

## Ian (Year 2)

Ian read aloud his first book, unaided, then proceeded to read another little book unaided. He then announced to his teacher that he would like to speak in sharing assembly this week.

### Why was this significant?

Ian had never before been willing to say anything in assembly, even when he had good work.

### Why did it happen?

Ian said *'I think I can do it now I can read.'*

**Type: attitude development** and **process skill**

## Comment

Ian has made progress by being able to speak in assembly, as well as by reading more confidently. Ian, like Emma above, gives another example where the development of confidence is interlinked for the child – he does not think he can speak to a large audience until he can read.

# Carlton (Year 2)

Carlton worked really hard for the first time and remained on task, using his wordbook well, as he wrote these two sentences:

> in our class room wen a ve got a computer AND we can write on The computer.

## Why was this significant?

Carlton had usually displayed time-wasting behaviour, and was not previously able to scan his wordbook unaided.

## Why did it happen?

Carlton said his Grandad had helped him to work every day during a month's holiday in Barbados.

## Type: attitude development and process skill

## Comment

Carlton's teacher noted that one-to-one attention helped Carlton to flourish, and that his progress needed to be reinforced by plenty of work with letters and sounds. His gain in confidence will help him to concentrate, so that his understanding of letters and sounds will continue to grow.

# Matthew (Year 3)

Matthew drafted his writing about space after a visit to the Planetarium.

> Space
> There are nine planets
> in the sollar system. stars
> are made out of Burning
> gas. The ~~more~~ moon looks
> Brite Becase the sit
> shines on the moon.
> There are stars whice
> make pattans and animals.
> The moon is made of
> Raok. It has holes.
> ~~The moon~~ Lots     of planets has a
> moon. The sur is very
> hot. pluto is made of
> frozen ice. and pluto
> is a very long way
> from the sun lots of stars
> make a Bear.

Reading it through with his teacher, he said *'It's a bit confusing to read because some of it's about planets and some of it's about stars and it's all mixed up together.'* At his teacher's suggestion, he underlined everything about stars in one colour, everything about planets in another, and everything about the moon in another. He then produced the final piece, reordered to help the reader, as well as with the spellings corrected.

> space.
>
> There are nine planets
> in the solar system. pluto
> is made of frozen ice and pluto
> is a very long way from
> the Sun. Stars are made
> out of burning gas. There
> are stars which make
> Patterns and animals. Lots
> of stars make a Bear. The
> Sun is very hot. The moon
> looks Bright Because the sun
> Shines on the moon. The moon
> is made of Rock. it has
> holes lots of Planets has
> a moon

## Why was this significant?

Although Matthew was used to identifying and correcting his spellings, this was the first time that he had reordered the ideas to make the content clearer.

## Why did it happen?

Matthew said *'It just seemed a bit muddled up.'*

## Type: concept clicking

## Comment

This example shows the importance of discussion with the teacher in the redrafting process. Matthew was able to realise that the sequence of ideas could be clarified. This type of redrafting, considering the ideas and how they are expressed, is ultimately more important than correction of spellings and punctuation and improvement of handwriting.

# Kwame (Year 3)

Kwame went with his class on a visit to Camden Arts Centre. He was asked a variety of questions and listened extremely well. He gave prompt answers to the workshop leaders and the quality of his answers showed a wide general knowledge, and an ability to be thoughtful and creative in his ideas.

## Why was this significant?

Kwame was usually quiet in class discussions, but was able to speak up in a totally different environment with complete strangers.

## Why did it happen?

Kwame said *'Because the stuff was good. It was nice.'* He liked the slabs of beeswax and the dress (the two different sculptures).

## Type: **process skill** and **social skill**

## Comment

Kwame showed his best speaking and listening skills in a context where he was genuinely interested and had something to talk about. As well as celebrating this achievement, Kwame's teacher noted that he should be given further opportunities to talk with different adults, and that it would be important to make sure he had time to answer in class discussions.

# Jess (Year 3)

Jess wrote his first piece of clearly written writing. His handwriting was dramatically improved and the paper was, for once, not dog-eared.

## Why was this significant?

Jess had always previously had handwriting problems.

The Greek Alphabet

| Capital letter | Small letter | Name | Sound |
|---|---|---|---|
| A | α | alpha | a |
| B | β | beta | b |
| Γ | γ | gamma | g |
| Δ | δ | delta | d |
| E | ε | epsilon | e |
| Z | ζ | zeta | z |
| H | η | eta | e |
| Θ | θ | theta | th |
| I | ι | iota | i |
| K | κ | kappa | k |
| Λ | λ | lambda | l |
| M | μ | mu | m |
| N | ν | nu | n |
| Ξ | ξ | xi | x |
| O | o | omicron | o |
| Π | π | pi | p |
| P | ρ | rho | rh,r |
| Σ | σς | sigma | s |
| T | τ | tau | t |
| Υ | υ | upsilon | u |
| Φ | φ | phi | ph |
| X | χ | chi | kh |
| Ψ | ψ | psi | ps |
| Ω | ω | omega | o |

Greek Scools.

Greek scools were private and only avalable to those who were rich enough to pay. only boys could go to shcool girls had to learn to rite and read at home. Thye used papyrus for paper but this was expensive and thue had to practise whith a stylus on wax. All thear words were Jorned together whethout any gapes. We know about Greek words because of Greek writing on pots. GREAT Brilliant.

## Why did it happen?

Jess said *'I wanted to please you.'* He had by then been in the class for half a term and had established a very good relationship with the teacher. He had previously been labelled a trouble-maker by his peers, and in this class was not always the one in trouble.

## Type: physical skill and attitude development

## Comment

This is another piece that shows the importance of confidence, a good self-image and good relationships in making significant progress. Jess's teacher has helped him overcome the obstacles to working well, so that his skills and understanding can continue to develop.

# Stefan (Year 3)

Stefan put his hand up in front of the whole class to answer a question about shopping.

## Why was this significant?

Stefan spoke very little English – just *'yes'*, *'no'* and simple sentences – and had never contributed to class discussions before.

## Why did it happen?

Stefan was not able to comment on his achievement himself. His teacher noted that he had been becoming more confident in group work, and also that the subject of shopping was one that related well to his personal experience, so he felt able to contribute.

## Type: social skill

## Comment

Stefan went on to do a piece of writing on the same topic. His teacher noted the importance of giving him subjects directly related to his experience to talk and write about.

# Fiona (Year 4)

Fiona was asked to finish an extract from a story which was chosen by the class teacher. The main characters had to be changed – 'Natile Johnson' instead of 'Katy Stuart' and 'nasty, cruel Jumble Josie' instead of 'Jupiter Jane'. The children were also asked to think of an interesting ending.

## Why was this significant?

Fiona's writing showed clearly the influences of her reading of different authors as she drew upon their styles in her own work.

## Why did it happen?

Fiona said *'I was able to think of new things. The book was exciting and I've got a good imagination.'*

The minute Natile Johnson ~~woke~~ opened her eyes she knew that this was the day she had been ~~waiting~~ Looking forward to for weeks. The day when the nasty, crule Jumble Josie would climb back into her spaceship and disappear forever, leaving Natile and her family in peace at last.* It was like a load suddenly falling off her back. That mean, disgusting Josie, who came to ruien her whole entire life was leaving! She yawaned and jumped out of bed. She had nearly fineshed getting dressed (she was looking for her new shoes) When there was a knock on the door "Hellow" Natile said "Who is it?" she said again "It's me, Jumble Josie who did think it was?" Natile dident

answer. She couldent belive her ears. "It must be my ears" she thought "I'll get them checked soon yes thats what it was". But just then that wreched voice came again "Helowow" anybody hereep?" Then Jumbel Josie marched in. Suddenly Natile came to her sences and managed to stammer "I..I th th thought y-you were go g go going today?" "Ah I decided I'd ~~stu~~ stay another day and get some more reserch done about earth don't mind do ya?" "n-not at a-a-all" Natile replied "Anyway" said Josie again "Whats the matter with you nat? got something in ya throut ave ya?" Natile dident say anything. She gave a faint smile at Jumble Josie and fled downstairs. Natile just couldent belive it oh why why why? did she have to stay just one more painful, hurting, terrible day!"

**Type: process skill**

## Comment

With older children, as well as with younger ones, the interplay between reading and writing can be seen. Here, Fiona's 'voice' as an author has been influenced by her reading.

# Carly (Year 4)

In a circle drama session, Carly asked for the cushion (which gave the right to speak) and voiced an opinion about bullying.

## Why was this significant?

This was the first time Carly had put forward a view without being asked.

### Why did it happen?

Carly said *'I feel very strongly about bullying'* and talked about the experiences of her older brother at secondary school.

### Type: social skill and attitude development

### Comment

Carly's contribution came about because she had something she wanted to say on a topic that was important to her. The experience of these circle drama sessions, in which the device of the cushion was used to structure the talk, gave Carly the security she needed.

# Sean (Year 4)

Sean asked if he could read to his teacher, and read the book *Featherbrains* beautifully, with lots of expression.

### Why was this significant?

Sean had been a reluctant reader who often groaned when asked to read aloud. He had a tendency to choose books which were too difficult for him.

### Why did it happen?

Sean said *'I really enjoyed that book.'* The book was new to the classroom and fitted in with the class topic on farming. His teacher had asked to borrow the book to read aloud the first chapter to the class as an introduction to the topic of battery farming.

### Type: attitude development and process skill

### Comment

This example shows just how important it is to provide children with a wide range of subject-matter and approach in their book corner, so that they have plenty of scope for finding something that catches their interest.

# Zara (Year 5)

For their topic on Beowulf, the children had poems about monsters read to them. Zara also read some poems on her own. They were then asked to write their own poem about Grendel. Zara wrote:

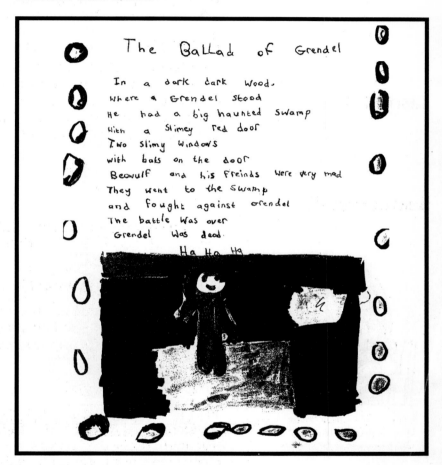

## Why was this significant?

Zara was a confident writer of stories, but this was the first poem she had written.

## Why did it happen?

Zara said *'I got the idea from reading poetry books about monsters.'* She had taken a keen interest in the poems she was reading and had clearly found in them a new source of enjoyment.

**Type: attitude development** and **process skill**

## Comment

Zara's new enthusiasm for poetry is a good demonstration of the way a teacher can broaden the range of children's reading by immersing them in a new genre and relating it to other thematic work. It is also another example of the way reading and writing go hand in hand in extending this range.

# Jason (Year 5)

Jason, like Zara above, was engaged in work about Beowulf. This is his comic strip:

## Why was this significant?

Jason is in the process of being statemented. He took a real interest in this work and completed it, a significant achievement for him.

## Why did it happen?

Jason was working with a group of boys who were all doing comic strips, and he said he wanted to do the same as them.

## Type: attitude development and process skill

## Comment

Jason's teacher noted the motivating effect of working in a group for him, and will give him more opportunities like this one.

# Jamilla (Year 5)

Jamilla, in the same class as Zara and Jason, made a 'Wanted' poster for Grendel (see over).

## Why was this significant?

Jamilla showed an exceptional interest and enthusiasm in this work.

## Why did it happen?

Jamilla said her brother had given her the idea for the poster on its brick wall background.

## Type: attitude development

## Comment

These three 'Beowulf' examples show clearly the power of literature to stir children's imaginations, and the value of immersing them in it and giving them time to develop a personal response. It is particularly noteworthy that the three children in the examples chose completely different forms for their writing – poem, comic strip, 'wanted' poster – each one trying out their writer's 'voice' in different ways in response to their reading.

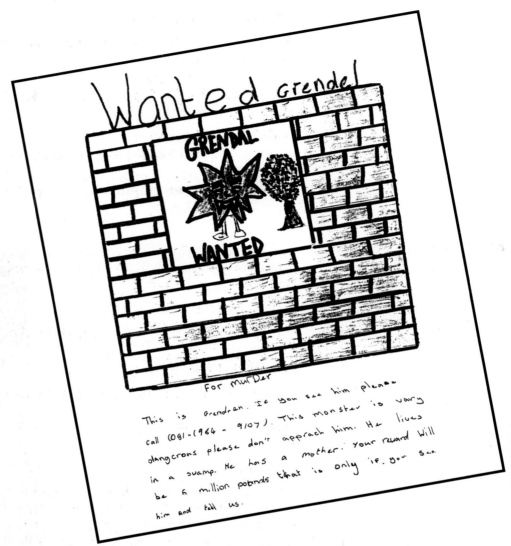

## Ben (Year 5)

Ben wrote a story, *'The Adventure of Bubble and Squeak'*, and redrafted it, taking on board some of his teacher's comments to make the story clearer and to answer some of her questions about incidents and events.

### Why was this significant?

Although Ben had been writing humorous, well-structured stories for some time, his teacher's attempts to get him to redraft adding detail and depth had so far been unsuccessful. This was the first time he had taken notice of audience reaction and redrafted.

## Why did it happen?

Ben said *'I took it home and mum saw the comments. She said I had to listen to them.'*

## Type: attitude development and concept clicking

## Comment

Now that Ben has understood about the importance of audience reaction, he needs to be encouraged to seek out audience comment for himself, perhaps by asking friends to comment on his drafts.

# Rebecca (Year 5)

Rebecca used capital letters and full stops in her free writing.

## Why was this significant?

This was the first time Rebecca had done this without help.

## Why did it happen?

Rebecca said *'I can see that it splits the story up.'*

## Type: concept clicking

## Comment

Rebecca has understood that punctuation helps the reader to follow the ideas in the writing, replacing the intonation and emphasis in spoken language. She is ready to apply this idea in learning about paragraphs and about other punctuation.

# Eleanor (Year 5)

Eleanor spent a considerable time drafting and redrafting her poem (see over).

## Why was this significant?

Eleanor had tended to produce her work in a rush and been very reluctant to revise and refine. This was the first time she had redrafted her work with attention to the significance and meaning.

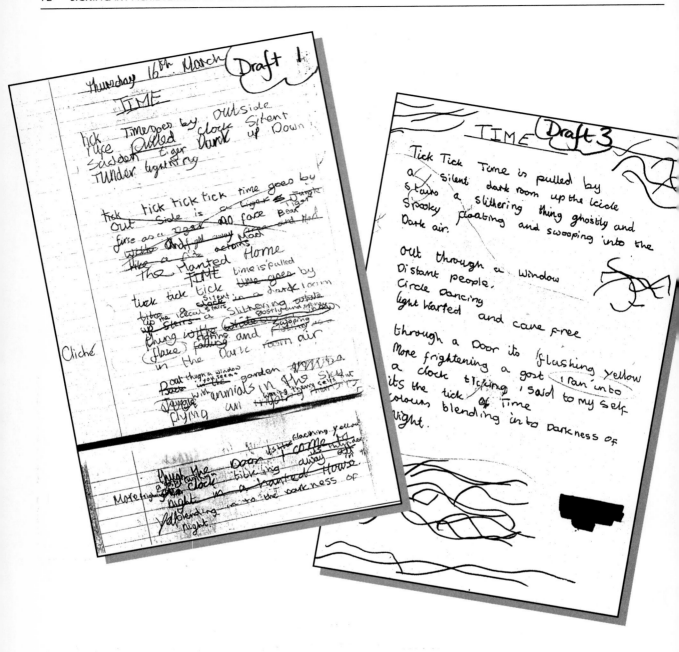

## Why did it happen?

Eleanor said *'I thought time would be a good idea. I like poetry, I like writing poetry. I wanted to get longer words and more meaning.'*

**Type: process skill and attitude development**

## Comment

Eleanor's work shows a real development through three drafts as she refines her vocabulary choices and tightens her structure. This is another example where immersion in poetry has helped children to produce their own. Her teacher recognised Eleanor's achievement by publishing the poem within the school.

# David (Year 6)

A student was taking David's Year 6 class, and was getting them to write poems about autumn. David sat and listened quietly and with interest, putting up his hand to answer questions. He wrote his poem in one go, took it straight to the student teacher and read it aloud. He copied the corrected version of the poem and worked with concentration.

*Autumn leaves*
*The wind is blowing. Leaves are falling off the trees.*
*It rains a lot and goes dark quick.*
*Orange leaves, brown leaves, red leaves and all*
*colours around the park floor*
*I kick it, a red leaf falls.*
*Leaves, leaves, leaves.*

### Why was this significant?

David has a statement of special educational needs. He has access to a support teacher most of the time (not on this occasion) and generally does not want to participate in anything the class is doing.

### Why did it happen?

David said *'I like the leaves in the park.'* When asked what had made him think of the last line of the poem, *'Leaves, leaves, leaves'*, he said that he had heard a poem where a word was repeated twice so he thought he would repeat it three times.

**Type: physical skill, social skill, process skill** and **attitude development**

### Comment

David's teacher noted that this student teacher had a particularly quiet and calm style, which David appeared to need. He also seemed to find this form of writing less threatening than story writing, where perhaps more is expected. These insights gave valuable pointers for helping David in the future.

# Sarah (Year 6)

Sarah wrote a long, well-structured story, paying particular attention to variety in her vocabulary choices. This is part of her first draft, showing the changes she plans to make to the final version.

### Why was this significant?

Sarah showed increased awareness of variety in vocabulary.

### Why did it happen?

Sarah was very involved in the story, and discussed her first draft with her teacher.

**Type: process skill**

Changing Places.

Chapter Two.

She gradually eased herself up on her bed. She looked at me, a look of blankness, on her face. Then, slowly and gently she asked "Did you do this?" "Of course I didn't. I didn't want this to happen." "Did you know this was going to happen?" She asked. "Well of course I didn't." I shouted. "Alright, no need to shout." "No need to shout? No need to shout?

"Phew. Thank ___
me." "And what's that supposed to mean?" "Nothing." Look, meet me outside Grubbs burger bar in 10 minutes." "Alright."

rest of the day. ___
"Hey, lets go to Horror House. It's said to be wild." "How much does it cost?" "£1.20 for us two and to go on as many rides as we want."

down and fell into a deep sleep. When I woke up I was a kid again. I had tea and went to bed. I lay down and looked at the ceiling. I felt good to be me."
The End

How am I going to be able to go to school like this? Then the phone went. "Wait a minute." she said. She ran to answer the phone "It's for you." I ran to answer ~~the phone~~ it. "Hello?" "I'm an adult." came the voice of ~~Dawn~~ Laura. "...so am I." "You are?" "Yes."

"Lets get a burge ___
the bar. Up at the counter our friend Fred, the waiter said "Hey, I'm sure I'v

The sign said. Sit down the ride of (your) life. We clambered in. The car streaked and jerked into ~~the life tunnel~~. Then Laura let

When you write up top copy, the next step in writing speech is to start on a new line when someone, or someone else, speaks.

patches
newspaper

## Comment

Sarah is becoming aware of her power, as an author, to make conscious choices about the words and sentence structures she uses. She knows that stories need to engage the interest of the reader, and that variety of style helps with this. Her teacher noted Sarah's ways of avoiding repeating the word 'said': *asked, shouted, came the voice of, called*. She has a variety of effective ways of expressing movement: *eased, froze, clambered, shrieked and jerked into life*, and she uses dialogue effectively to move the story forward. Her teacher's note about setting out speech on the page in her final draft is a well judged indication of the next step forward for this capable young writer.

# Callum (Year 6)

Callum used a dictionary to correct a draft of a story independently. The next time he wrote a story, he used the dictionary as he wrote, and produced this story with correct spellings the first time.

## Why was this significant?

This was the first time Callum had used a dictionary independently in his writing.

## Why did it happen?

Callum said *'I've got a new dictionary.'*

## Type: conceptual development and process skill

## Comment

This is an important step to independence, as Callum can now monitor his own work and produce correct spellings without help from the teacher. This means that he has to *know which words he has to check* as well as being able to use his new dictionary easily.

# Mark (Year 6)

Mark read with concentration for the whole of the class reading session and had to be prised away from his book to go on to other work.

## Why was this significant?

Mark was not a very confident reader, had little access to books at home and did not enjoy reading, especially sustained silent reading. In the class reading session, he had often been fidgety, changing his book frequently and staring out of the window.

## Why did it happen?

Mark said *'It's a good book, I really like it, it's gory!'*

## Type: attitude development

## Comment

Mark's teacher noted the importance of providing books – even gory ones – to grip 11-year-olds. This is also an example that shows the influence of other children. This book had been given to Mark by a member of an exclusive 'reading club' formed by some children in the class who brought in books to share. Mark's need for attention and esteem from this group may have helped as a spur to his reading.

# Daniel and Rachel (Year 6)

Both Daniel and Rachel produced poems of exceptional quality.

### The secret

I have a secret,
To me it is very special,
My secret is visible, but untouchable,
It uses force to move itself.
The colour that it is,
Moves your mind far away
But keeps your body
In a still, blood-rushing position.
Its frozen, crackly form slips through everything,
Like it was the skin of your teeth.
Its shadow creeps stealthily up your spine,
Freezing it to ice.
My secret can humanly magnetise itself
To any shape,
Taking its nerves away.
Some people say my secret is bad, dirty and dangerous,
As it may well be,
But only to others, not to me,
To me,
It is very special.

### Pylons invading the land

It's almost an attack,
An attack from mankind itself.
The bases of the pylons grate the soil violently,
As the human race lands them down
To transport their power,
Unaware that they are putting
One step of force,
Against Nature.

Defenceless, the nature-living animals
Flee in distress from the danger,
Yet some do not survive the strike.
Then, the human wizardry begins,
The electricity along the pylons
Like blood rushing through an artery in a human body
The attack is soon over,
And survivors can slowly cut off the panic.

### Environment and Pollution

Oil tankers spilling into seas
The energy saved from primeval trees.
Petrol vapours filling the skies
Choking fumes stinging our eyes.
Hamburger packets litter the street
Crunched up cans beneath your feet.

If we are not careful
Soon you will see
There won't be space
For you and for me.

### War

I look out
Only to see
A grey, plain scene
Not a single tree.
Just broken hearts
Lost families

Death creeps by all,
Silently.
Famine swoops past all,
Hungrily.
Hate, anger and greed fit the scene,
Perfectly.

Both cries of anger
And of pain
Pierce the air
Bombs grasp the remains of land and limbs
A piercing scream breaks out.

## Why was this significant?

Although the children had been identified as good writers, they had not produced this level of sophistication before.

## Why did it happen?

This work was the result of a 'poet in residence' programme. The poet performed his poems to the school and then worked with small groups of children, giving them ideas for poems and helping them revise their ideas. The children knew they were working towards a performance, with the poet, of their poetry at the end of the residency. In addition, the school was publishing a book containing the best poetry which would be on sale in the village shops.

Daniel said the poet had given him lots of ideas and had suggested the titles he used.

Rachel said that at first she had thought that the poet gave her the ideas, but in fact neither title had been suggested to her. The war poem related to her work in history, and the other idea 'just came'.

## Type: process skill

## Comment

These poems show exceptional accomplishment in their use of vocabulary and imagery, and in the sureness of touch with which they are shaped. They bear witness to the way good teaching can bring about significant achievement by able children which is quite remarkable. The poet-in-residence programme gave the children motivation, a reason for writing, an audience, and the opportunity to talk about their writing as a skill and an art.

This collection of classroom events has brought out the great variety of achievements that can be significant for different children in different classes. It has also brought out the wide range of factors that have given rise to those achievements.

There have been plenty of examples of sound, well-thought-out teaching, following the principles described in Chapter 2, clearly taking children forward. But there have also been many examples which were completely unpredictable – the influence of other children, factors from outside school, and difficulties in one area causing a lack of confidence in another, for example. One teacher even described a little girl who seemed to produce a significant achievement every time she wore a particular hairband!

In all these cases, however, it is clear that teachers have learned a great deal by talking to children about their achievements, and reflecting on what they say. The thoughtful points noted by the teachers in this chapter show the value of this approach in knowing children better and working with them to build on their achievements.

Overall, the examples in this chapter have shown a progression from the beginnings of reading and writing amongst the youngest children to the breadth, confidence and self-monitoring abilities of the oldest. The next chapter will look in a more structured way at the kind of progression that can be expected through the primary years in speaking and listening, reading and writing.

# 4 Development and Progression in English

## Introduction

In Chapter 3, there were many examples of particular steps in the development of individual children as their language abilities increased. This chapter sets these individual steps in the context of the lines of development that can be seen, typically, as children progress through the primary years. In Chapter 2 (pages 31–2) these lines of development were sketched out as a table. Here, the aim is to put some flesh on those bones.

For each of reading, writing and speaking and listening, there are two 'case studies', one of a child early in the primary years, the other of another child towards the end of the primary years. Rather than highlighting particular significant achievements, as in Chapter 3, an overview of each child's performance is given. These case studies are then related to the table in Chapter 2, showing progress FROM the early years TO the end of Key Stage 2.

# Reading

## Stacey, *age 6*

Stacey is reading aloud to her teacher from the picture book *But Martin!* Her teacher introduces the names of the characters in the book. Stacey reads most of the text independently, making full use of her understanding of the story, familiarity with the characters, and the repetition in the sentence structures. When she gets stuck, she is mainly reliant upon these strategies to help her with unknown words. She reads *'gold'* instead of *'golden'*, and *'floppy'* instead of *'floaty'*. When she comes to *'began'*, she cannot make a prediction from the meaning of the story, and tries to sound out the word. She says the sounds *b*, *e* and *g*, but cannot put these together and needs her teacher's help to read this word. At this stage, she is not yet skilled at looking at the detail of the print to help her to read unknown words.

As she reads, she comments from time to time on the story and the pictures, pointing to the green spaceman Martin with long antennae on his head instead of hair. She says she enjoyed the story and it would be fun if a spaceman came to her school – she would ask him if he wanted to play skipping with her.

When Stacey has become familiar with a book like this, she will choose it from the book corner to share with a friend or read by herself. There are a number of other story books, some of them from a reading scheme, that she knows well in this way. She rarely picks up an unfamiliar book to look at. When her teacher reads an information book, she listens with interest. She joins in with nursery rhymes and poems when her teacher reads them, but her own choice is for familiar story books.

**FROM . . .**

### . . . using some reading strategies

Stacey makes good use of cues from meaning but cannot yet use phonics fluently.

### . . . enjoyment of familiar books

Stacey loves books, but does not yet have the confidence to move beyond familiar story books.

### . . . understanding stories

Stacey follows the meaning of the story and relates the happenings in the story to her own experience.

### . . . reading with literal understanding

Stacey understands the events in *But Martin!*

**TO ...**

**... having a good grasp of all reading strategies, and using them fluently as needed**

Laura reads fluently both silently and aloud, and has integrated all her strategies in order to gain meaning from the text.

**... enjoyment of a range of types of book**

Laura enjoys stories, poems, information books and instruction books. She understands that books can be read in different ways for different purposes. She can cope with long texts as well as picture books and has the confidence to try unfamiliar types of text.

**... discerning character, plot, theme, style**

Laura understands that the characters and events in the story have been created by an author, and can comment on the way this has been done. She relates the book to her own experience, but is also able to distinguish the characterisation and to comment on this in detail.

**... reading with deeper understanding of implied as well as literal meanings**

Laura's description of Bobbie's character shows that she has understood aspects that are implied by Bobbie's words and actions, and by the events in the story.

# Laura, *age 11*

Laura has brought a selection of books that she has read recently, to discuss in her regular reading conference with her teacher. They include the novels *The Witches* and *The Railway Children*; a short paperback guide to drawing cartoon figures; the *Eyewitness Guide: Skeleton*, which she has been using recently in her science work; the poetry book *I Like That Stuff*; and the picture book *Dr Xargle's Book of Earthlets*, used in recent drama sessions.

Laura chooses *The Witches* and the cartoon book as her current favourites. She describes how she has been spending time perfecting her drawing of a cartoon cat called Spike, her own invention. She says *'I like this book because it shows you exactly how to start off, but then leaves it up to you to make up the details'*. She had read the story of *The Witches* when she was younger, but chose to read it again because her friend Vicki had just read it. She says *'I started it at school and then took it home and read it straight through. My mum had to make me put it down at bed time.'*

Her teacher asks how *The Witches* compares with her previous home reading, *The Railway Children*. Laura thinks for a while, and then says that *The Railway Children* took longer to read than *The Witches*: *'It wasn't so fast moving but it had more in it – you sort of got to know the people better because the author put in lots of detail about what they said and did.'* The teacher follows this up by asking Laura about the characters in *The Railway Children*. She replies *'Bobbie is my favourite character because she's very kind and quite grown-up. She has to grow up really, to be a help to her mum when her dad's away.'*

Laura also talks about the way the pictures and words are organised to give information in the *Eyewitness Guide*, about the humour in *Dr Xargle* and about some of the poems she has read. She reads her favourite poem aloud to her teacher, bringing out the meaning in the expression of her voice.

# Writing

## Steven, *age 5*

Here is the writing Steven produced after going out into the school wild garden to observe snails:

*I am waiting to see the snail the snail comes out*

Steven wrote this without help from his teacher, and read it back clearly. When his teacher asked where it said *'snail'*, Steven pointed to the letter *'s'*.

Steven's piece shows that he understands how writing can be used to recount a personal experience, and that he is beginning to work out how letters correspond to spoken words. He knows the words *'I'*, *'am'* and *'the'*, has a good idea of consonant sounds and is making a guess at vowel sounds. He does not yet separate his words with spaces, and does not know how full stops can help the reader by showing separate ideas. His letter shapes are recognisable, but not yet regular in size.

Most of Steven's writing, like this piece, recounts his own experiences. He writes about things that happen to him at home at weekends and holidays, and about his direct experiences in school. When his teacher asks him to write a story, using a well-known book as a model, Steven will write a sentence of commentary, usually describing a single picture or event in the story – he does not yet write a series of events.

**FROM . . .**
**. . . writing for oneself**

**. . . writing as an immediate form of self-expression**
Steven's writing is an expression of a direct experience he has had.

**. . . using language unreflectively**
Steven's writing is spoken language written down.

**. . . writing in familiar forms**
most of Steven's writing is a recording of his personal experiences at home or at school.

**. . . forming letters recognisably**
all of Steven's letters are clearly recognisable.

**. . . knowing some spelling patterns**
Steven knows how to spell some words and uses consonant sounds to make good guesses at others.

**. . . not understanding what punctuation is for**
Steven does not use full stops or capital letters to separate his ideas.

**TO . . .**

**. . . writing for others, judging how to interest and entertain them**
Chris paces his story well, and puts in detail, description and conversation to set the scene and draw his characters.

**. . . using note-taking, brainstorming, drafting and revision as appropriate**
Chris uses all these approaches to writing.

**. . . knowing that the choice of words can be controlled for effect**
Chris is aware of the way in which turns of phrase establish a well-known character, and uses dialogue to suggest arrogance.

**. . . willingness to try out a variety of types of writing**
Chris can write story, poetry, discussion and persuasive writing.

**. . . varying handwriting style according to purpose**
Chris normally writes quickly in joined-up script, but uses capitals and decorative handwriting styles in his poster.

**. . . knowing how to spell most words**
with a few slips, Chris knows most of the spelling patterns and many irregular words.

**. . . using all forms of punctuation fluently and appropriately**
Chris's story shows capitals, full stops, question marks, commas, speech marks, paragraphs, and dots to indicate hesitation.

# Chris, *age 11*

This is an extract from Chris's own Hercule Poirot story, written after reading several of the books:

*Hercule Poirot made his way to the Inspector's office. The door was the kind you would find in detective movies with misted glass and 'Inspector Jenson' written in big black letters across the middle of the door.*

*'Ahhh, Monsieur Poirot.' Jenson eyed over the detective, stopping and staring when his eyes reached Poirot's amazing moustache. 'I've heard a lot about you. Do you think you will be able to live up to your reputation?'*

*'You are, how do you say . . . sceptical. Well, Monsieur, people who doubt the grey cells of Hercule Poirot are always proved wrong.'*

The story, *'Death under canvas'*, is ten pages long. Clues are introduced in the course of the narrative which are brought together in Poirot's set-piece speech at the end, in which the murderer is unveiled.

Talking about his story with his teacher, Chris identifies the main characteristics that he has used in re-creating Poirot – his arrogance, his use of bits of French in conversation, and his 'catch phrase' – *'little grey cells'*.

Most of the spellings in the story are correct: mistakes include *'untill'* and *'actully'*. There is a secure grasp of paragraphing and a variety of punctuation used correctly.

Other writing in Chris's portfolio includes: a poem, which is a pen portrait of a friend and which went through three drafts; a poster for the school summer fair, using a variety of letter styles and sizes; and a discussion of the play facilities in the school playground, produced as part of a group after a brainstorming session.

# Speaking and Listening

## Aslan, *age 6*

Aslan, who speaks Urdu at home, is playing with two other children in the class shop. The shop sells fruits and vegetables that the children have made, and has a till with real coins. Aslan takes the role of the shopkeeper. His conversations include:

6 *Now I'm the shopkeeper. I'm putting the money in here.*
*Would you like to buy some apples?*
*How many?*
*That's 15 pence. Give me 15 pence.*
*Thank you. Goodbye. See you tomorrow.* 9

He is clearly aware of the other two children, and takes the role of the shopkeeper appropriately and with confidence. After a few minutes, one of the other children asks to be shopkeeper, and Aslan happily adopts the role of customer.

Aslan also participates confidently in other play activities, talking with two or three other children as he plays. He is happy to work in a small group with the teacher and a few other children, and to talk one-to-one with his teacher. In class discussions, Aslan follows what is being said, and very occasionally contributes a sentence or two of his own experiences.

There is one other Urdu speaker in the class, and these two children will sometimes play or share a book together, talking in Urdu. Whenever other children are part of the group, however, Aslan speaks English. He knows that his home language is Urdu, and describes how he uses it to say hello to his mum and dad when he gets home from school.

**FROM . . .**

**. . . talking with small numbers of familiar children and adults**
Aslan is confident with his teacher and with a small group of children, but is more reserved in class discussion.

**. . . asserting a point of view and listening to others**
Aslan interacts well with the other children.

**. . . involvement in imaginative play**
Aslan takes the familiar role of shopkeeper appropriately.

**. . . talking for oneself**
at the beginning, Aslan's words seem to be 'thinking aloud', describing his role to himself as he gets into it.

**. . . using language unreflectively**
Aslan has some awareness of his own language, as he is able to describe the use of his two languages at school and at home.

**TO . . .**

**. . . talking with known and unknown people**
Daniel's radio programme is addressed to an unknown audience who will be unfamiliar with the subject matter.

**. . . adjusting ideas, making suggestions**
Daniel listens to Yasmin's idea, thinks it is a good one, and repeats it so that the others do not ignore it.

**. . . taking a variety of roles, including some unfamiliar or unsympathetic ones**
Daniel adopts the pro-zoo role, researches it, and presents it consistently using appropriate arguments and forms of expression.

**. . . talking for others, judging what information they need**
Daniel shows clearly that he is explicitly aware of the need to explain the background of the interview to the audience.

**. . . knowing that the choice of words can be controlled for effect**
Daniel's argument shows good use of persuasive language: *'valuable service'*, *'hunted to extinction'*.

# Daniel, *age 11*

Daniel is working with a group of children to prepare a taped 'radio programme' presenting the case for and against zoos, as part of work on the environment and endangered species. His conversations include:

❛ *We've to make sure they know who's talking in this interview. Someone needs to introduce it. They need to say, like, 'and here are two people who disagree about it.* ❜

❛ *Listen – Yasmin's idea was good – we should start with the interviewer asking each of them to say what they think.* ❜

❛ [in role] *You've got to realise what a valuable service we zoo keepers are doing for animals and the environment. Hundreds of species would have died out if it weren't for zoos. Animals can breed safely there, but in the wild they would be hunted to extinction.* ❜

These extracts show Daniel explicitly considering the needs of his audience and able to listen to and take account of the suggestions of others. In role, he chooses vocabulary appropriate to the character he is playing, and sustains the position he is arguing consistently.

The final radio programme is played to the other Year 6 class, and a lively debate ensues.

Daniel tends to be an 'organiser' in classroom activities, taking the lead and making suggestions, but is still able to listen to others. Class discussions have included sensitive topics such as friendship, families and bullying, and Daniel contributes thoughtfully and listens to others.

# 5 Some Common Questions Answered

This chapter deals with the common questions that emerged as teachers began to focus on significant achievement in English.

## ▶ Does this fulfil the statutory requirements for assessment and for OFSTED?

Yes. The statutory requirements are that assessment and record-keeping must be done in relation to the core attainment targets, but the amount of assessment and recording and the form of records is entirely up to teachers, taking account of good practice and manageability. The SCAA/DFEE Assessment Arrangements state that collections of evidence are not required, nor tick lists for each child against the criteria of the National Curriculum. You may receive guidelines from LEA advisors or inspectors asking you for some of these things, but the actual statutory requirements are as outlined here.

The significant achievement system fulfils the statutory requirements, with the tracking matrix ensuring tracking against the attainment targets of the National Curriculum.

## ▶ How can I be sure I am recording achievement across the whole of the National Curriculum?

Concentrate on the Programmes of Study, rather than the attainment targets. In English, these set out the range, key skills, and aspects of standard English and language study that are expected at Key Stages 1 and 2. You need to plan work with your class so that class work, group work and individual work combine to cover the Programmes of Study at a level appropriate to the children. Many teachers have found that they need to pay particular attention to the 'range' section – the variety of reading and writing that children do – as it is easy to get stuck with just one or two types of text (stories, for example).

▶ **How many times do you have to see significant achievement to write it down?**

You need to define the significance. For instance, it might be significant for a child to hold her pen properly for a short period of time and should be recorded as such, even though she may go back to holding it wrongly afterwards; it is at least a first step. The next significant achievement for that child would probably be when you notice that she is now holding the pen properly all the time. Recording significant achievement has a formative purpose – it aims to support the teacher in planning the next step for the child. This is quite different from the summative tracking of attainment in relation to the old Statements of Attainment. Then you were being asked to consider children's abilities against set criteria, which took no account of an individual child's progress towards certain goals.

▶ **I have some bright children in English who always seem to fulfil my learning intentions. Is this really significant achievement?**

This is a common comment by teachers when they first start tracking significant achievement. The first thing to do is congratulate yourself that your monitoring system (i.e. the tracking matrix) has helped you to identify this as an issue. Fulfilling your learning intentions may indeed constitute significant achievement for some children, but brighter children should be showing as much significant achievement as less able children. However, if a particular group regularly and easily do all that is expected, this suggests that children are not really being stretched and are working well within their limits.

▶ **How can I get children to talk constructively in a group? They seem to need to turn to me all the time when they are working, and just chat when they are left to themselves.**

Children will not suddenly start to have constructive group discussions because you have asked them to. They need to learn what they are being asked to do, how to go about it, and how to know whether they are doing it well. So, first, accept that it is going to take time and don't give up after the first unsuccessful attempt. Try these steps:

**Pick a suitable activity.** If the main purpose is to develop group collaboration, don't make the content of the discussion too demanding. Give children a clear task to undertake as a group, with a clear outcome that they all understand. Set a time scale for the discussion, and make sure they all understand that.

**Talk to them about the discussion.** Make it clear that you are expecting them to work on the task by talking together, and that they should listen to one another's ideas and try to involve everyone.

**Ask them how it went.** Make it clear that you care how the discussion went, as well as how the task was accomplished. Talk about listening, consideration, working together. Try to identify some significant achievements and reward them on the spot.

**Try it again soon.** Remind them of how well they did the first time and encourage them to improve.

▶ **What do you do about a child who is not showing any significant achievement?**

This shows you have a good monitoring system that is bringing such children to your attention. First of all, perhaps it is just that you have not noticed what the child is doing. Teachers pick up children's responses in a variety of ways, through questioning, class discussion, children's recording, or observations of how children work. However, some (often quiet) children seem invisible. It is worth planning to watch the child more closely. Track the child through the day or week. What does the child do? Is the child involved in discussion or activities? Who does the child work with? Where does the child position him/herself? Who does he or she talk to? Does this lack of progress spread across the curriculum? Is the child making small steps forward rather than dramatic leaps that demand attention? Talk with the child during activities – does the child understand the purpose of the tasks that have been set? Ask the child about likes and dislikes, and where he/she feels confident and lacking in confidence. This may give you some clues about what is going on. Involve other colleagues and any support staff who work with the child. Talk with parents, if appropriate.

Sometimes this investigation will produce some kind of answer – for example, a need for support or extra challenge in a particular area, the need to rearrange class groupings or tackle problems in the playground. It may suggest areas of special interest or confidence you can build on. In reading and writing, too, it is as well not to be too impatient. Progress in language is often not steady. Some children seem to need to 'take things in' for a long time before they can start doing it for themselves. So they might join in with reading big books as a class for a long time before they can read any words themselves. Then, progress may be rapid, as they finally 'take off'. This is rather like a baby learning to talk: they understand for a long time before they produce anything themselves. On other occasions where this lack of progress is persistent and these everyday processes are not throwing any light on the problem, you will need to involve special needs staff and procedures in a more long-term discussion of the child's progress.

▶ Will a reading scheme help me to track progress?

Reading schemes can be helpful, as they provide a structured approach where the demands of each book are clearly set out for the teacher. But, as Chapter 2 makes clear, children need much more than can be provided by a scheme alone: a range of styles; high quality text and illustrations; interesting use of vocabulary; a wide range of subject matter; and scope for choice. Some of the examples in Chapter 3 show children whose interest is only aroused by very particular books in very particular circumstances. So schemes are fine, used judiciously, but must take their place as part of a rich mix, and must themselves be of high quality.

▶ How do I track progression in languages other than English?

It is not usually possible to keep a clear track of progress in other languages if you do not have access to that language yourself. But other home languages do contribute to children's attainment in English, and it is as well to find out as much as you can about them. Talk to the child, and to the parents, and older brothers and sisters if there are any. Find out what language or languages are spoken, and in what circumstances at home; whether the child knows stories, songs and rhymes in the home language; whether he or she is learning to read and write in the home language. This will form the basis for occasional follow-up conversations so that you build up a fuller picture of achievements.

## ▶ How can I support and assess bilingual pupils?

Many of the suggestions in Chapter 2 provide a vital starting point in supporting bilingual pupils. First and foremost it is important that bilingual pupils feel that their language and culture are valued in school, and that they have work that is appropriately challenging. In planning and organising activities, it is helpful to consider the following:

◆ Is there scope for bilingual pupils to use their first language?
◆ In what ways does the activity build on existing knowledge and understanding?
◆ How can the activity be introduced so that it is accessible to all? – consider the use of diagrams, demonstration, models, practical resources, gestures, pictures, tapes, display.
◆ Which key words would it be useful to translate and reinforce? Make sure you identify, use and reinforce the same words each time, so that children can follow the strands in your talking.
◆ How will bilingual pupils contribute and record? Can they do this in their first language?
◆ Is the grouping supportive – allowing use of first language, including a supportive friend or a competent user of English?
◆ How can the activity extend the child's linguistic ability?

## ▶ How do you get time to talk to the children?

It is important that the idea of significant achievement is *not* seen as something *separate* or *added on* to normal classroom practice. Discussion about learning intentions and significant achievement needs to be built into the usual times we talk to children – when we introduce tasks, talk with children about their work, handle feedback sessions, manage class sharing time, mark work, etc. Then the question becomes: How do you get time to talk to children in general? Teachers spend most of their time talking to individual children in the classroom, whether they are sitting in a group or answering questions or being brought finished work. These are the natural times for an assessment dialogue to take place; it is a matter of simply changing the emphasis of the things you say, including questions about the child's views on progress in terms of the shared learning intentions (see Chapter 1) as well as the usual management or supportive general statements.

▶ **Do you need to moderate significant achievement, so that we all mean the same thing by it?**

The purpose of moderation processes is to establish common definitions of each level of the attainment targets within the context of children's work, to ensure greater confidence in teachers' own assessments at the end of the Key Stages.

Moderation is only appropriate where there is a set of criteria, as in the National Curriculum level descriptions, which will be used to create levels for each child at the end of each Key Stage.

In tracking significant achievement, however, although your basic framework for most children will be the National Curriculum Programmes of Study, there can be no benchmarks defining stages of significant achievement. There is no need to embark on moderation of significant achievement because each teacher is in the best possible position to decide what constitutes significance for each child. One child's range of significant achievements may only take them a small step along the development set out in the programmes of study, whereas another child might have an equal number of significant achievements, but end up much further along the way. Very often your criteria for significant achievement will not be found in the programmes of study anyway, but are significant because they help the child along the continuum of learning in all its aspects.

It is, however, very useful to get together as a staff and share examples of significant achievement so that you can build up a clearer picture of what achievement might look like for a particular child or in a particular subject area. (See Chapter 6.)

### ▶ What do you show parents?

The child's record of significant achievement provides an invaluable focus for discussion at parents' evenings. It gives a picture of the whole child, shows developments that have taken place across the curriculum, and indicates the next steps that need to be taken. It can be very useful in helping parents to appreciate what constitutes progress in each subject. Schools also need to continue to produce end-of-year reports which summarise progress over the previous year.

Some schools place a marker (red felt pen mark) in the top right corner of any page of a child's workbook which has a significant achievement comment on it. This gives easy and instant access to significant work in children's books, both for parents and teachers.

### ▶ How would you carry out agreement trialling with the National Curriculum level descriptions?

The level descriptions are intended to be used by applying 'best fit'. The idea is that you consider the whole range of a child's achievements and decide which level for each attainment target best fits a child's achievements. This should not be an exact fit, but rather the one which best corresponds to what a child can do overall.

In order to develop a common interpretation of the levels, one strategy is for each teacher to bring one child's work for the agreed attainment target to the agreement trialling meeting, with a page of prepared notes summarising the kinds of things the child can do which are ephemeral (not written down by the child but corresponding to the criteria in the level descriptions). In pairs or fours, teachers take one child's work at a time and decide what level is most appropriate and why it cannot be the next level. Groups move around the room looking at the work until all groups have seen all children's work (about four children's work for a one-hour meeting). At the end, the groups compare their judgements, opening the debate to decide the majority opinion. Any problems which occur about decisions or interpretations of the level descriptions can be taken up with local education authority advisers or SCAA subject officers.

There are, of course, other approaches to agreement trialling.

## ▶ What would a School Portfolio look like?

The purpose of the school portfolio is to provide evidence of the school's agreed interpretations of the levels. The idea is that the work agreed at agreement trialling meetings is simply placed in a folder of some kind. This can then be shown to moderators, parents, governors, new teachers or any other interested parties.

If you decide to moderate using whole collections of work from one child, the portfolio could consist of plastic punched wallets, one for each level of the core attainment targets, so that lots of work from one child can be shown for each level. This work would obviously have to be put into the folder at the end of the year when the child is no longer using it, so a reference sheet could be placed in the wallet until then.

The portfolio could also consist of a large file, with work simply stored in the file between dividers for each attainment target and for each level.

There should be, for each collection for each level, a brief note about the level decided and why it did not fit the next level up. It should also include the date of the meeting.

## ▶ What about the end of Key Stage and the allocation of levels?

At the end of the Key Stage your planning records, the child's work, your marking, the record of achievement and your informal observations of their progress will give you ample evidence on which to base your judgements of a child's level. These sentiments are echoed in the SCAA/DFEE Assessment Arrangements booklets.

# 6 Getting Started

The previous chapters have discussed ways of promoting and identifying significant achievement in English and have examined examples from the classroom. The question then is: How do you get started? How can you begin to track significant achievement in your class or school? How do you develop the language activities going on to create the conditions for significant achievement to occur? This chapter offers some suggestions based on the experiences of teachers who have been involved in courses on significant achievement.

## Getting started: some general principles

In planning the introduction of any change or new development, such as tracking significant achievement, the following general principles are useful.

### Build on what you are doing already

Many elements in the approach to tracking significant achievement discussed in this book are not new. The approach draws on many developments in primary practice over the last few years, for example:

◆ a more consistent approach to planning;
◆ the increased recognition of the need to clarify learning intentions;
◆ the involvement of the *child* in assessment, for example through the *Primary Language Record* (CLPE 1988) or the use of self-assessment sheets in mathematics;
◆ development of pupil profiles and Records of Achievement;
◆ the discussion of dimensions of learning, as for example in *Patterns of Learning* (CLPE 1990).

As a result, there may be many aspects of your current practice that you value and can build on. It is therefore important to begin by reviewing what you do already as a school or class, and considering how it could be extended or modified.

## Start small

Trying to introduce a complete change in practice overnight is a daunting prospect and rarely effective. Starting small gives teachers the chance to experiment with different approaches and techniques, share problems and evolve an overall system that fits their own school policies and situation. You could begin with a small pilot project on significant achievement: tracking significant achievement in your class for a few weeks, concentrating on one area of the curriculum or involving a small group of interested teachers. Some teachers have introduced the idea of significant achievement to their schools by working with interested colleagues and then gradually involving the whole staff.

## Begin with areas of strength and extend outwards

In taking on any new idea, building on areas of strength gives you the best chance of success. Many teachers when starting to consider significant achievement have begun by concentrating on language development, as this is the area in which they feel most confident and have the clearest view of children's progress. They have then extended the same approach to other areas of the curriculum.

## Make time for regular review

As new practices are introduced and implemented, ideas often change and develop. Further suggestions emerge or unanticipated problems occur. People can become discouraged by difficulties or lose focus once the initial enthusiasm wears off. Planning opportunities to review what has happened and share experiences can enable teachers and children to refine their approach, regenerate commitment and have a sense of their own progress with this new venture.

# Getting started: examples of practice

Over the last year teachers have shared with us the differing ways in which they have introduced the idea of significant achievement in their classes and schools and begun to develop their practice in English. The following suggestions are based on their ideas and experiences.

## Getting started with your class

In the early stages, teachers reported that they had tried to promote and identify significant achievement in their classes by:

### Focusing more explicitly on learning intentions

◆ clarifying learning intentions at the planning stage;
◆ sharing learning intentions with the children in a variety of ways – through talk, writing, display and questioning;
◆ planning time to review learning with the class and individuals.

### Introducing the idea of significant achievement to the class

◆ talking with the class about significant achievement;
◆ sharing examples of children's work over the last year, since they came to school or from the infants/nursery – discussing how the examples differ: reading more difficult books, different types of book, understanding about character and setting, writing longer stories, stories that begin and end well, stories that readers find exciting, spelling better, neater or joined-up handwriting, speaking to the whole school in assembly;
◆ making decorated sheets and folders to record and store examples of significant achievement;
◆ setting up a display or notice board about significant achievement, linking this to learning intentions;
◆ establishing a sharing time for children to talk about things they are proud of.

### Tracking significant achievement

◆ monitoring significant achievement for a month, examining the pattern for individuals and areas of the curriculum (using the grids from Chapter 1);

◆ identifying individuals or areas of the curriculum that need further attention;
◆ tracking the significant achievements of 3–4 children in detail.

## Taking time to discuss children's work

◆ making notes of significant achievement on children's work *at the time*;
◆ referring back explicitly to learning intentions;
◆ indicating not just *whether* the work was good or not, but *why* and *in what ways*;
◆ drawing attention to positive examples of work both during and after sessions.

## Involving children in decision-making

◆ sharing ideas for planning at the start of a project or activity;
◆ discussing improvements in classroom resources and their organisation;
◆ explaining the need to talk with groups or individuals about their work;
◆ talking about how children can help and support each other.

## Considering the whole child in context

◆ focusing on the development of skills as well as knowledge and understanding;
◆ recognising the importance of attitudes and approach to learning;
◆ examining classroom groupings more critically;
◆ considering the involvement of parents.

## Reviewing progress

◆ encouraging children to identify their own significant achievements;
◆ getting feedback from children about the effects of focusing on significant achievement – many noted a considerable increase in confidence and self-esteem;
◆ noting individuals *not* making significant achievement;
◆ sharing successes and progress with the class.

# Getting started with the school

Teachers used a number of different strategies for introducing the idea of significant achievement in their schools. They:

◆ introduced the idea of significant achievement using the framework described in Chapter 1;
◆ shared examples of significant achievement from their own classrooms or the course;
◆ asked teachers to bring their own examples of significant achievement to a staff meeting, sharing ideas and difficulties and identifying common patterns;
◆ reviewed current practice in planning, assessment and record-keeping;
◆ discussed ways of building a focus on significant achievement into aspects of current practice, e.g. planning cycle and proformas, current observation and sampling procedures or systems of record-keeping;
◆ trialled the approach for half a term, identifying groups/areas of the curriculum where significant achievement is often not observed;
◆ planned INSET to focus on areas of concern, for example mathematical or scientific investigations, extending able pupils, and assessing bilingual learners;
◆ exchanged examples of progress regularly, both formally and informally;
◆ discussed what should be passed on to the next teacher, each teacher bringing a child's Record of Achievement to a meeting and swapping records with a colleague, deciding what would be useful.

# Developing English in the classroom

In trying to promote significant achievement in English teachers indicated that they were:

## Looking for where children can make choices

◆ trying to give the children a choice in something previously chosen by the teacher;
◆ letting children follow up their own ideas whenever possible; encouraging discussion about choices;
◆ asking children to tell a friend/their group what they have chosen and why;
◆ encouraging children to ask each other about choices.

## Looking for audiences and purposes

◆ finding new audiences for the children to write for;
◆ finding new audiences for the children to talk to;
◆ talking about purpose in writing: Who are we writing for? What are we telling them? Why? What do they need to know?;
◆ talking about purpose in reading: What is this author writing for? What is he/she telling us? How is he/she organising the information?

## Giving status to reading and writing

◆ checking that reading is given attention in its own right;
◆ checking that writing is not just used in the service of other subjects.

## Raising the level of demand

◆ asking more difficult questions when discussing reading: Why? How? How did they feel? Does this remind you of anything else?

## Organising resources and displays

◆ reviewing book corner books;
◆ introducing new text types and talking about them;
◆ looking at different writing materials;
◆ planning stimulating displays of children's work.

## Discussing discussion

◆ asking how the discussion went;
◆ asking if everyone felt involved.

## Involving bilingual learners

◆ checking that they know all the languages children use outside school;
◆ learning greetings, numbers, etc, in other languages.

## Involving parents

◆ setting up a classroom display of significant achievement in language;

- displaying a planning poster with the range of reading and writing and learning intentions clearly indicated;
- sharing examples of significant achievement in English with parents, both formally and informally

Above all, by listening to children and encouraging them to offer their ideas, as time went on teachers reported seeing far more examples of significant achievement.

*Only you and your immediate colleagues can decide how best to apply the principles involved in tracking significant achievement in your own class or school. It is important that you let these principles guide the style and formats you adopt for recording purposes, rather than making the recording system the first point of reference. And although the approach to assessment outlined in this book more than satisfies statutory and inspection demands, some educationists and others will always ask for paper-and-pencil statistics, in order to satisfy their own agendas. We must make sure that they do not lead us to focus on meaningless marks on paper, when our duty is to help to further children's **learning** to the best of our ability.*

- conc + intro tomorrow → finish patch 2.
                        → start patch